I0518999

VICTOR
OR
VICTIM

VICTOR
OR
VICTIM

GEORGE SWEET

NEBP
NORTHEASTERN BAPTIST PRESS

Bennington, Vermont

Victor or Victim

Copyright © 2023 by George Sweet

Published by Northeastern Baptist Press
        Post Office Box 4600
        Bennington, VT 05201

All rights reserved. No part of this book may be reproduced in any form without prior permission from Northeastern Baptist Press, except as provided for by USA copyright law.

Scripture taken from Holy Bible, New Living Translation.
Copyright © 1996, 2004, 2015 by Tyndale House Foundation.
Used by permission of Tyndale House Publishers, Inc.
Carol Stream, Illinois, 60188.
All rights reserved.

Cover design by Leason Stiles

Softcover ISBN: 978-1-953331-32-8

This book is dedicated to my wife, Gina.
Thanks for joining me on life's great adventure.

TABLE OF
CONTENTS

Chapter 1
Choosing to Be a Victor or a Victim
1

Chapter 2
Adam and Eve: Playing the Blame Game
5

Chapter 3
Cain: A Slave of Emotions
11

Chapter 4
Abram: Self-focus Leads to Victimhood
17

Chapter 5
Esau: A Victim to His Own Dealings
23

Chapter 6
Joseph: Victimized but Not a Victim
31

Chapter 7
Aaron: A Victim of Peer Pressure
39

Chapter 8
Nadab and Abihu:
The Cost of Ignoring God's Instructions
45

Chapter 9
Achan: When the Spoils of Victory Lead to Defeat
51

Chapter 10
Caleb: A Life-long Devotion to Victory
55

Chapter 11
Samson: Trading Victory for Victimhood
61

Chapter 12
Naomi: Hard Times Give Way to Hope   67

Chapter 13
Hannah: The Power of a Heart-felt Prayer   71

Chapter 14
David: Waiting on God's Promise   77

Chapter 15
David: Repenting Like a Victor   83

Chapter 16
Elijah: Eroding Faith Slips into Victimhood   89

Chapter 17
Elisha: Trusting in the Unseen   95

Chapter 18
Nehemiah: Focusing on Godly Success   101

Chapter 19
Job: Victory Despite Losses   107

Chapter 20
Shadrach, Meshach, and Abednego:
Living with a Win-Win Attitude   113

Chapter 21
Daniel: Victorious in the Face of Workplace Conflict   119

Chapter 22
Jonah: Finding Misery in God's Blessings   125

Chapter 23
Jesus: The Ultimate Victor   131

CHAPTER 1

Choosing to Be a Victor or a Victim

Every time we face challenging or difficult circumstances, we make decisions that impact our identity. The issue is: Do we let our difficult circumstances define us, or do we overcome our difficult circumstances? We choose to be either a victor or a victim. Choosing to be a victor leads us to persevere through the circumstances in such a way that we develop admirable character qualities. On the other hand, choosing to be a victim leads us to surrender to the circumstances in such a way that our character faults become obvious. We often hear people either on the TV or in real life complaining about the problems in their lives but claiming no personal responsibility for their problems. They are suffering from their own bad decisions but blame someone else. Granted, sometimes we suffer due to the actions of someone else, but not all our suffering is the fault of others. Sometimes our suffering is self-inflicted.

Regardless of whether your circumstances are self-inflicted or not, you can choose to think and act as a victor or a victim. My family has many stories revolving around my sister Stacey that are good examples of the victor versus victim mindset. Stacey was born with Down Syndrome, and the doctors told my parents that they should put her in an institution – there was not much hope for her. My parents refused to do so and brought her home. Each of us worked with Stacey to help her develop in different areas. My major role was to be her sports coach, and I guess I was successful because she has many Special Olympic trophies and medals. At one track and field competition years ago, Stacey and I approached the softball throw event area. The volunteer handed Stacey a softball and then moved about ten yards away from her. He did not realize that Stacey could throw 2-3 times that distance. She looked at me with a confused expression, and I said to the man, "You are going to have to scoot back." He replied, "Young man, I have been doing this all day. I think I know what I am doing!" Stacey looked at me again, and I said, in not my proudest moment, "Aim at his head." She whizzed the ball by his ear, he dove to the ground, and then scooted back. Stacey got the gold – clearly the victor.

In this book, the lives of twenty-four people whose lives are described in the Old Testament will be examined to discover the right and wrong ways to deal with the circumstances of life. The chapters ultimately lead up to and culminate in the greatest Victor of history, Jesus Christ. Some of the people serve as a positive role model, and others show us how not to respond. Along with each biblical character or characters, a contemporary situation will be discussed to apply the truths of the Scripture to the situations in our lives. The chapters have been kept short, but not so you can finish the book quickly and add it to your list of books read this year. Instead, this is so you can interact with the points without being overloaded with too much information. It is my hope that this book will help you live as a victor, not a victim.

CHAPTER 2

Adam and Eve:
Playing the Blame Game

The idea of living as a victim is not a new issue; there are examples of people playing the victim card going all the way back to the beginning. Adam and Eve were perfectly created and placed in the most exquisite place that has ever existed on this planet – the Garden of Eden – and they still played the victim card. Why would they act like victims when their own foolish decisions were clearly at fault?

Their fall into victimhood began when they started to listen to the counsel of Satan more than the counsel of God. After a brief discussion about the established boundaries in the Garden of Eden, the devil told Eve, "'God knows that your eyes will be opened as soon as you eat it, and you will be like God, knowing good and evil.'" (Genesis 3:5, NLT).

This is an amazing con job because the devil convinced Eve that what she really needed in life was a good dose of evil. The devil told her that though she already knew what goodness was like, she needed to know the flip side of goodness. She followed the devil's words more than God's words and her physical senses more than her spiritual discernment: "The woman was convinced. She saw that the tree was beautiful, and its fruit looked delicious, and she wanted the wisdom it would give her. So, she took some of the fruit and ate it. Then she gave some to her husband, who was with her, and he ate it, too." (Genesis 3:6). As a result, Adam and Eve, as well as the rest of us, would clearly know the impact of evil. It is clear that the decision to ignore God's boundaries was not forced on them; it was a choice that they made. They were not victims in this situation. They became a victim of the consequences of their choices.

Later, God confronted the couple and asked a location question: "'Where are you?'" (Genesis 3:9). The question was not asked in order for God to discover their location; He knew where they were. The question was asked so that they could know where they were in terms of their relationship with Him. The following paragraph is a historical transcript of their conversation.

Adam: "I heard you walking in the garden, so I hid. I was afraid because I was naked," (Genesis 3:10).

God: "Who told you that you were naked? Have you eaten from the tree whose fruit I commanded you not to eat?" (Genesis 3:11).

Sin was a quick teacher. Instead of answering the question honestly, Adam invented the blame game that is still very common today. The blame game has its roots in an individual being unwilling to accept the consequences for their actions. At the soul level, a person refuses to be wrong or at blame for something wrong. Instead of taking personal responsibility, the finger is pointed to someone else as the reason for the problem. It is a worldview that claims, "it's not my fault; someone else made me do it."

In this case, Adam pointed his finger at two other beings: his wife and his Creator, saying, "'It was the woman you gave me who gave me the fruit, and I ate it,'" (Genesis 3:12). Adam was saying that he was the victim here because God gave him this woman that had led to his downfall. His thinking had shifted dramatically from the time that he had exclaimed, "'This one is bone from my bone, and flesh from my flesh! She will be called woman, because she was taken from "man"" (Genesis 2:23). When confronted with his actions, Adam now viewed the woman as the reason for his problems, instead of being a God-given helpmate. In this way of thinking, he also blamed God for creating her and putting her in his life.

The victim blame game continued as God spoke to the woman. After He confronted her, she responded, "'The serpent deceived me... That's why I ate it,'" (Genesis 3:13). This statement was more in line with the truth, but her victim's mindset tried to remove her responsibility from the decision she made to eat the forbidden fruit. Victims are always looking for someone else to be at fault.

The next big question is: Did Adam and Eve continue to live life as victims, or did they start to take personal responsibility for their lives? We are not given many more personal details about Adam and Eve, except for the birth of their sons. Perhaps they refused to play the victim anymore, but it seems that they may have passed their victim mentality on to their children, as we will see in the next chapter.

Before we move on, though, let's think about situations that we might face in which we make a poor decision and then try to turn ourselves into victims instead of fools. Oftentimes we are embarrassed when we get caught doing something foolish, so to restore some semblance of pride, we play the blame game. I remember an incident from junior high school when one of my friends asked me if I thought our math teacher looked pregnant. I was not sure if I could tell if she was pregnant or not, but it was too good of a story to keep to myself. So, over the next several days, I started a whispering chain of gossip around the classroom that seemed harmless until the math teacher caught wind of what was going on. The big problem was that our math teacher was not married and was quite upset about this rumor. She also proved to be a good detective because she traced the rumor back to me, and in a moment of weakness I blamed my friend, claiming that I was just passing on what I had heard from him. The math teacher forgave me, but unfortunately my friend did not, and our friendship ended that day. Playing the blame game may temporarily get you out of trouble, but in the end, it will cost you. In this case, it cost me a good friend.

CHAPTER 3

Cain:

A Slave of Emotions

Sometimes we are victims of our own emotions, especially the emotion of anger. The best advice on dealing with anger is found in the Bible: "Be angry, and yet do not sin; do not let the sun go down on your anger, and do not give the devil an opportunity," (Ephesians 4:26-27, NASB). The wisdom in these verses directs us to control our feelings of anger instead of being controlled by them. It is not always easy, but it is the best way to avoid the trouble an outburst of anger causes.

Adam and Eve's first two children, two boys named Cain and Abel, had a sibling rivalry that ended in a terrible tragedy. A turning point in the lives of the two boys came as they each gave an offering to the Lord. Cain was a farmer, so he brought an offering of the fruit of the ground (Genesis 4:3). Abel brought an offering of the firstborn of his flock and of their fat portions (Genesis 4:4a). The Bible tells us: "The LORD accepted Abel and his gift, but he did not accept Cain and his gift," (Genesis 4:4b-5a). As a result, Cain became very angry – the kind of anger you can identify by one look at a person's face (Genesis 4:5b).

God saw the raging anger in the face of Cain and asked him two questions. First, he asked him, "'Why are you so angry?'" (Genesis 4:6a). Just as God had asked Adam and Eve, "Where are you?" after they sinned so they could realize their situation, here God asked Cain to identify the reason for his anger so that he could learn that he had no valid reason to be angry with Him. Second, God asked Cain, "'Why do you look so dejected?'" (Genesis 4:6b). Some people's emotions are evident from their facial expressions, and this was true of Cain. Notice that God did not rebuke him for being angry. Rather, He was asking Cain questions about his response to his anger.

Then the Wonderful Counselor said to Cain, "'You will be accepted if you do what is right. But if you refuse to do what is right, then watch out! Sin is crouching at the door, eager to control you. But you must subdue it and be its master,'" (Genesis 4:7). God was telling Cain that he had a decision to make. He could acknowledge the anger and control it, or he could let the anger take over his thinking and it would control him. God told him that if he did not correctly respond to his anger, being a slave to his emotions was going to destroy his life. Cain ignored God's advice, and instead he attacked his brother and killed him.

After the murder, God confronted Cain about his actions toward his brother: "'Your brother's blood cries out to me from the ground,'" (Genesis 4:10b). Due to the fact that Cain was a willing participant in this crime and not really a victim, God punished him: "'Now you are cursed and banished from the ground, which has swallowed your brother's blood. No longer will the ground yield good crops for you, no matter how hard you work! From now on you will be a homeless wanderer on the earth,'" (Genesis 4:11-12).

Part of having a victim mentality is being shocked and overwhelmed by any consequences that may arise from a misdeed. A victim tries to turn the tables to get you to feel sorry for them. This is the strategy used by Cain: "'My punishment is too great for me to bear! You have banished me from the land and from your presence; you have made me a homeless wanderer. Anyone who finds me will kill me,'" (Genesis 4:13-14). Notice that Cain added some consequences to his sentence not mentioned by God, such as God hiding His face from Cain, and God setting Cain up to be murdered. God guaranteed that neither scenario would be true by protecting Cain as he lived as a vagrant and a wanderer of the earth (Genesis 4:15).

Like Cain, sometimes we become victims of our emotions – they hijack us and take us places that we did not plan on going. This happens because somewhere in the process, we make a decision to let our emotions have control over our lives. Instead of mastering our emotions, we become a slave to them.

Let's take a look at someone who lets their emotions and bad choices push them into claiming the identity of a victim – we will call this character "Mark." Mark was raised by parents who had strong morals, although they did not go to church often. His parents did the best they could to teach him the difference between right and wrong in his thinking and actions. Mark's friends described him as an easy-going guy that did not get angry often. As Mark moved out on his own, he began to frequently drink alcohol. At first, he was careful only to drink at home because his parents had told him many horror stories about the perils of drinking and driving. But Mark had much insecurity as a young man, and he used these identity struggles to justify the drinking. He rationalized it as a good thing for him because the alcohol temporarily erased the insecurity from his mind. As time went on, his tolerance to alcohol increased, so he drank more, but he would find moments in which the alcohol was gone but the insecurity remained. Depression would set in, and he would drive to the store for more beer so that he could continue to self-medicate. One time after a night of drinking, he was still struggling with feeling like a failure, so he went back to the store for a third time to buy more beer. On the way to the store, he got stopped by the police and was found to have a blood alcohol level of .12% and was arrested for driving under the influence (DUI). As a result of his DUI conviction, his driver's license was suspended.

Mark's personality began to change after he lost his license. His laid-back personality was replaced by an attitude that flipped back and forth from hopelessness to rage. He lost his job because he had trouble getting to work since he could not legally drive. He would complain to anyone who would listen that it seemed like everyone was out to get him and it was unfair that he lost his license when he had not hurt anybody. His drinking increased during his time of unemployment, as did the amount of blame that he spewed out.

Who was to blame for the predicament in which Mark found himself? Mark caused this problem for himself. Mark will likely remain in his misery as long as he plays the role of a victim to his emotions. Like Cain, Mark saw the consequences of his actions as unreasonable, and sought to convince others that he was the victim. Unlike Cain, there is hope for someone like Mark, as can be seen from the testimonies given weekly at Celebrate Recovery[1] meetings. But first he must accept personal responsibility for his situation. When he sees the problem as his own doing, then he is at the beginning stage of mastering his emotions instead of being mastered by them.

---

1 Celebrate Recovery is a Christ Centered 12-Step Recovery Program. You can learn more at https://www.celebraterecovery.com/.

CHAPTER 4

Abram:
Self-focus Leads to Victimhood

You might think that a hero can easily avoid being plagued by a victim mentality. However, only one hero has lived a perfect life. Our heroes often vacillate from victor to victim. For example, God chose to use a man named Abram in a heroic way. God told Abram, "'Leave your native country, your relatives, and your father's family, and go to the land that I will show you. I will make you into a great nation. I will bless you and make you famous, and you will be a blessing to others. I will bless those who bless you and curse those who treat you with contempt. All the families on earth will be blessed through you,'" (Genesis 12:1-3).

In heroic fashion, Abram was willing to leave everything and most of his family behind and follow God's leading – a new start at the age of 75. Imagine getting a message from God in which He told you to start heading west until you reached the place where He wanted you to live. Furthermore, when you ask for the place's name so you can connect your GPS to it, God says to you, "I will tell you when you get there." Without a doubt, acting on such a calling requires a heroic faith in God. Indeed, Abram is known as one of the champions of the faith (Hebrews 11:8). When Abram arrived in the land of the Canaanites, God told him, "'I will give this land to your descendants,'" (Genesis 12:7a). Abram built an altar and worshiped God in his new homeland.

It appeared that nothing could derail the great faith of Abram...until a famine struck the land. Hard times often purify our faith by revealing the impurities hidden within it. Abram had a weak spot: He was insecure about people's responses to his wife. So, as they entered Egypt, he said to his wife Sarai, "'Look, you are a very beautiful woman. When the Egyptians see you, they will say, "This is his wife. Let's kill him; then we can have her!" So please tell them you are my sister. Then they will spare my life and treat me well because of their interest in you,'" (Genesis 12:11-13).

Do you see how our hero's focus changed? Suddenly he was not seeking to follow God but to save his neck from a hypothetical situation. In his mind, he was able to justify denying his marriage and having his wife taken to be a member of Pharaoh's harem in order to save his own life. Abram became a victim to his fears and could only think of his own possible troubles. The shift from victor to victim happens quickly when a person becomes self-centered.

God was not OK with this situation. He "sent terrible plagues upon Pharaoh and his household because of Sarai, Abram's wife," (Genesis 12:17). When Pharaoh found out, he was furious with Abram and ordered him to leave Egypt. We would hope that Abram learned a valuable lesson and never repeated this same lack of moral judgment, but when he later entered the Negev, he followed the same pattern of sin for the same selfish reason. Some may argue that he used this ruse to become wealthy, but it cost him his reputation, which is more valuable than riches.

Abram's failure can be strangely encouraging to us when we realize that even the great father Abraham (as he later became known) failed to live consistently as a victor. Some people have also stumbled from the mountaintop to the valley like Abram. For example, let's imagine that you are an extremely gifted high school student. You are well respected by your peers and teachers for your academic abilities. However, what people do not know about you is that you are very insecure about your math skills. Even though you have always gotten good grades in math, you have this nagging feeling that a bad math grade is going to keep you out of the college that you desire to attend.

While you are taking geometry, the teacher gives you a take-home test and tells you that you can use the book to help you answer the questions, but you cannot get someone to help you answer the test questions. You are convinced that this is the dreaded math assignment that is going to sink your college dreams. So, you convince one of your friends who is good at math to write in the test answers for you. They agree to your plan, and you turn in the test thinking that your plan has succeeded. However, your math teacher not only knows geometry but notices her students' hand-writing styles. As she is grading your test, something seems wrong to her, so she finds one of your previous assignments that she had in a folder and compares the handwriting. The two writing samples are obviously different. The teacher confronts you, and you admit that you had a friend take the test for you. Your geometry grade is impacted by your zero score on the test (as a result of cheating), but the more significant consequence is the damage to your reputation as a student.

Sometimes the decisions we make that we think will help us end up hurting us. In our own wisdom we develop plans, but God tells us in His Word: "There is a path before each person that seems right, but it ends in death," (Proverbs 16:25). It is much better to rely on God's wisdom: "Trust in the Lord with all your heart; do not depend on your own understanding. Seek his will in all you do, and he will show you which path to take," (Proverbs 3:5-6). Keeping your eyes on God and His ways marks the path of the victor; focusing on yourself at the expense of others marks the path of the victim.

CHAPTER 5

Esau:
A Victim to His Own Dealings

Sometimes we suffer hard times due to our impatience, which is usually fueled by our need for instant gratification. This is not a modern problem. One of the grandsons of Abraham, Esau, struggled with the need for instant gratification, and it cost him a lot.

Esau had a twin brother, but the two men were much more different than they were similar. Esau was an outdoorsman; Jacob liked to stay in the tents. Esau was the pride of his father; Jacob was a momma's boy. There was tension and competition between the two boys, highlighted by this fateful encounter:

"One day when Jacob was cooking some stew, Esau arrived home from the wilderness exhausted and hungry. Esau said to Jacob, 'I'm starved! Give me some of that red stew!' (This is how Esau got his other name, Edom, which means "red.") 'All right,' Jacob replied, 'but trade me your rights as the first-born son.' 'Look, I'm dying of starvation! said Esau. 'What good is my birthright to me now?' But Jacob said, 'First you must swear that your birthright is mine.' So Esau swore an oath, thereby selling all his rights as the firstborn to his brother, Jacob. Then Jacob gave Esau some bread and lentil stew. Esau ate the meal, then got up and left. He showed contempt for his rights as the firstborn," (Genesis 25:29-34).

What catches your attention in this passage? Here are some things that I notice.

1) Either Esau was an ineffective hunter and gatherer, or he went on a longer outdoor excursion than he had anticipated. He was an outdoorsman but came back to the tents on this day with nothing to eat. Or, it is possible that God prevented him from any success in the hunt to set up this situation.

2) Esau felt so hungry that nothing else in life mattered to him other than getting some food – regardless of the cost. This is an obvious case of impatience and a desire for instant gratification. Esau would not take time to make a meal for himself but bartered a meal from his brother.

3) Esau expressed his apathy toward the rights and privileges of the first-born. In his state of impatience, Esau did not rationally consider the offer made to him by his brother. No matter how good the food tasted, Esau made a bad deal. Later he would regret his impulsivity in this matter.

4) Jacob was persistent in getting what he wanted even if it meant that he had to take advantage of his brother. Obtaining his brother's birthright was not a spontaneous act as much as it was the work of one brother scheming against another. The story of the brothers' relationship shows that Jacob lived up to his name: "Deceiver."

Let's fast forward a few years to the end of the life of Esau and Jacob's father. Traditionally, the father gave a blessing to his children, especially his first-born. Isaac knew that his time was short, so he told Esau to kill and prepare one of his favorite meals, so that "'then I will pronounce the blessing that belongs to you, my firstborn son, before I die,'" (Genesis 27:4b). Isaac's wife, Rebekah, overheard this conversation, (remember that Jacob was a momma's boy), so she came up with a plan to deceive her husband into giving his blessing to Jacob instead of Esau. Rebekah's plan worked, and Isaac gave Jacob his blessing (while thinking he was blessing Esau): "'From the dew of heaven and the richness of the earth, may God always give you abundant harvests of grain and bountiful new wine. May many nations become your servants, and may they bow down to you. May you be the master over your brothers and may your mother's sons bow down to you. All who curse you will be cursed, and all who bless you will be blessed,'" (Genesis 27:28-29).

Almost catching Jacob in the act of impersonating him, Esau approached his father with the meal he had prepared so that he could receive his father's blessing. Isaac and Esau realized that Jacob (although it was primarily Rebekah) had deceived them. Esau cried out to his father, "'Oh my father, what about me? Bless me, too!'" (Genesis 27:34b). His father responded, "'Your brother was here, and he tricked me. He has taken away your blessing,'" (Genesis 27:35). Esau's response was interesting: "'No wonder his name is Jacob, for now he has cheated me twice. First, he took my rights as the firstborn, and now he has stolen my blessing. Oh, haven't you saved even one blessing for me?'" (Genesis 27:36).

What do you notice about these statements? Here is what stands out to me.

1) Jacob's reputation as a deceiver was well known in his family. It was no secret that Jacob was not the kind of man to be trusted. He looked out for his own welfare without caring about how his actions impacted others.

2) Esau admitted that Jacob had obtained his birthright – the privilege of the first-born. Jacob possessed the birthright because Esau sold it to him for a bowl of stew. Although this was a strange transaction, it was a well-documented trade.

3) After admitting the transferal of the birthright to Jacob, Esau still wanted the blessing of the birthright that he had traded away. Esau acknowledged that he had traded his birthright to his brother, but he wanted the deal to be made null and void now that it was time for the privileges of the birthright to be fully activated.

Isaac did give Esau a blessing, but it was obviously inferior to the blessing received by Jacob: "'You will live away from the richness of the earth, and away from the dew of the heaven above. You will live by your sword, and you will serve your brother. But when you decide to break free, you will shake his yoke from your neck,'" (Genesis 27:39-40). After this encounter, Esau seethed with enough anger that his focus turned to murdering his brother.

How did Esau lose the blessing of the firstborn? Was he a victim? He tried to play the victim card, but ultimately, he gave away his birthright in a moment of impulsivity. Jacob had a role in the transference of the blessing, but ultimately it was Esau who made the decision to give away his birthright. Like Esau, sometimes we make an impulsive choice that costs us, and instead of owning our foolishness, we blame others to the point that we seek vengeance on them. My dad once gave me a valuable piece of advice: "when you mess up, admit it and work to make it right." This advice has come in handy more times than I can count. For example, one time I made a mistake at work, and it affected the head boss in a negative way. When the mistake was pointed out to me, I had the memo retyped and took it up to the head bosses' office. I was escorted into the office by one of my supervisors who was chastising me for my mistake. The head boss looked at the new memo as I explained to him the corrections. He smacked the desk in front of him, and said, "That is outstanding! Good work!" I was so glad that I followed my dad's advice because I was able to move from being a victim to being a victor.

CHAPTER 6

Joseph:
Victimized but Not a Victim

Sometimes the way that we approach victory can lead us to the path of victimhood, and the way that we approach defeat can lead us to the path of victory. The critical question is: What defines us?

Jacob had many sons, but the most memorable one was named Joseph. "Jacob loved Joseph more than any of his other children because Joseph had been born to him in his old age. So one day Jacob had a special gift made for Joseph – a beautiful robe," (Genesis 37:3). In response to Joseph being the father's favorite son, his brothers grew to hate him to an extent that they did not want anything to do with him. It appears that the blessings of the father's love created scorn toward Joseph in his brothers' hearts.

It does not take enormous discernment to realize that a person in Joseph's predicament should not flaunt any superiority over his brothers. However, Joseph lacked such insight. For example, he told his brothers about one of his dreams: "'Listen to this dream... We were out in the field, tying up bundles of grain. Suddenly my bundle stood up, and your bundles all gathered around and bowed low before mine,'" (Genesis 37:6-7). This is an easy dream to interpret and does not reflect well on his brothers' future relationship with Joseph. To make matters worse, Joseph had a similar dream in which the moon and eleven stars bowed down to him, which he shared with his family as well. His father rebuked him for sharing the content of the dream but continued to ponder its meaning. His brothers were jealous of him and began to scheme against him.

One day, Joseph's father asked him to check on his brothers and the flock. When his brothers saw Joseph approaching, they "made plans to kill him," (Genesis 37:18). Instead of killing him, they opted to take off his coat of many colors and throw him into a pit, to die of dehydration. Eventually, they decided to sell him to some traders and fake some evidence that would indicate his death to their father. Clearly, in this situation, Joseph was not the family champion, but an exploited commodity. When the traders arrived in Egypt, they sold Joseph to the captain of Pharaoh's bodyguards.

Joseph was not the type of person who identified as a victim, so even though he had been victimized by his brothers and was now a slave, he didn't give up or lose hope. Despite his circumstances, he rose in status to be his owner's personal servant and was made the superintendent of the man's house and possessions (Genesis 39:3-4). Even though this was not the path that Joseph thought his life would follow, he seemed content in his situation. However, his master's wife began to lust for him and tried several times to seduce him. One time, when nobody else was around, she grabbed him and begged him to sleep with her (Genesis 39:11-12a). He ran away so quickly that she was left still holding his garment.

The master's wife made up a story about Joseph trying to rape her, and Joseph was sent to prison. Sometimes we can overcome bad circumstances once in a while, but when difficult circumstances cascade over one another, it gets difficult. One night I was watching one of those TV shows in which contestants are put through intense challenges. As stress is piled onto stress, the confidence of each person is impacted. In many situations, a person's resolve to continue erodes in the face of a series of struggles. The same phenomenon can be experienced in a person's spiritual life. Faith in God remains steady after a struggle or two, but a longer sequence of hard times can threaten a person's faith. Joseph's faith in God was frequently tested by his circumstances.

Yet even in Joseph's difficult back-to-back trials, "the LORD was with Joseph in the prison and showed him his faithful love. And the LORD made Joseph a favorite with the prison warden," (Genesis 39:21). Just as before, in his downtrodden situation in which it would have been easy to play the part of the victim, Joseph rose to the top: "Before long, the warden put Joseph in charge of all the other prisoners and over everything that happened in the prison. The warden had no more worries because Joseph took care of everything. The LORD was with him and caused everything he did to succeed," (Genesis 39:22-23). Even in prison, Joseph overcame the struggles, living with the mindset of a victor. His steadfast and tested character traits were recognized by the warden, and he was shown favor.

While Joseph was in prison, God gave him the ability to interpret dreams for two prisoners. Both dream interpretations were fulfilled, but Joseph remained locked in prison. The prisoners that he had helped had agreed to mention his help to Pharoah. One prisoner died, as the dream had prophesied; the other prisoner forgot all about Joseph. Then Pharaoh had a dream from God that haunted him, and none of his advisors could interpret it. At this point, the cupbearer who had had his dream interpreted by Joseph remembered him and mentioned his ability to interpret dreams to the Pharaoh. So Pharaoh called for Joseph and told him the dream, (which was actually a pair of similar dreams). Joseph was able to interpret them and save the region from a devastating famine. As a reward, Pharaoh made Joseph the second-in-command of Egypt. Now the man who had overcome being sold into slavery by his brothers, being falsely accused of rape by the wife of his master, and being forgotten in prison was placed in a leadership position to save the people of Egypt from starving to death. The one who could have languished in a prison as a victim of the system was now a victor over his circumstances and the Prime Minister of Egypt.

The story was not over, though -- in fact, the plot thickens. During the famine, Joseph's brothers, who did not know what had happened to Joseph after they sold him, came to Egypt to buy grain. They did not recognize Joseph, but he recognized them. He sold them grain but kept one of the brothers in prison as collateral until they returned with their youngest brother, Benjamin. The brothers returned with Benjamin, but still failed to recognize Joseph. Eventually he revealed his identity to his brothers. Because he identified God's victorious leading in his life, he displayed no hard feelings toward his brothers who had severely mistreated him, saying, "'But don't be upset, and don't be angry with yourselves for selling me to this place. It was God who sent me here ahead of you to preserve your lives,'" (Genesis 45:5). Joseph reveals an important principle of thinking like a victor: Look for the hand of God in all your circumstances.

After more time passed, Joseph's father came to Egypt for a complete family reunion. After Israel (or Jacob) died, Joseph's brothers thought that Joseph would finally seek his vengeance on them. They made up a story to convince him to be nice to them, but Joseph had no thoughts of vengeance because he saw the hand of God in his circumstances. He told them, "'Don't be afraid of me. Am I God, that I can punish you? You intended to harm me, but God intended it all for good. He brought me to this position so I could save the lives of many people,'" (Genesis 50:19-20).

When we feel like we have been victimized, we have several options to choose from, but only one of them is good. We can decide that we need to get vengeance against whoever has wronged us, but that never has any positive effects. Consider how different Joseph's story would have been if he had escaped from Potiphar's house, returned to his family, and killed them all by burning their houses while they were sleeping in them. Think of the vast number of people whose lives would have been immeasurably worse if Joseph had sought vengeance against his brothers.

Or, instead of getting vengeance, we could just give up on life. Imagine Joseph, curled up in a corner of a prison cell – refusing to eat, refusing to talk, and refusing to even move. His life story would have ended tragically: alone, betrayed, and forgotten in a prison cell. He could have lived as a victim wallowing in his misery instead of the victor who would save many people from dying during a famine.

At some point in life, someone will probably give you a reason to seek vengeance on them. Before I knew Jesus, I lived by the popular motto: "I don't get mad; I get even." If you hurt me, I hurt you. What changed this pattern? Jesus changed me from the soul out. Those old fleshly patterns of sin may want to come out, but I don't have to be controlled by my sinful desires because Jesus has set me free from them. I can choose to show the grace of a victor when I used to show the anger of a victim. So can you.

If any person in history had a right to hold tightly to the victim card, it was Joseph. But he identified himself as a servant of God and not a slave to others' treatment of him. Because of this, even in the worst of situations, Joseph was a victor.

CHAPTER 7

Aaron:
A Victim of Peer Pressure

Sometimes the reason we do the things we do has nothing to do with our personal desires or a carefully thought-out life plan. Sometimes we do things due to the power of peer pressure. When we are controlled by peer pressure, we go along with what others want us to do because we want to avoid confrontation. If we make a habit of following others' plans for our lives, then we can feel powerless and hopeless – everything is decided by someone else. This is a characteristic of thinking like a victim.

Aaron was the brother and ministry assistant to Moses. He had been with him from the time when they first told Pharoah, "'This is what the LORD, the God of Israel, says: Let My people go so they can hold a festival in My honor in the wilderness,'" (Exodus 5:1b). He had seen the plagues that God sent on Egypt. In fact, God had turned his staff into a serpent as a sign that He wanted His people released from Egypt. Aaron had seen God's grace on the people of Israel during the first Passover (Exodus 12). He had seen God part the Red Sea so the Israelites could escape Pharoah's army (Exodus 14). He had seen God provide water out of a rock in the desert. He had seen many miraculous works of God for His people.

When Moses went up Mount Sinai to receive the commandments of God, he left Aaron as one of the people in charge. It was in this context that the Israelite people became restless. They said to Aaron, "'Come on... make us some gods who can lead us. We don't know what happened to this fellow Moses, who brought us here from the land of Egypt,'" (Exodus 32:1). In this encounter, we see the fickleness of human loyalties. Extending this thought, we should question whether the thinking of our peers—which is often fickle, false, or foolish—is worth following. Essentially the question is: Are we going to be responsible for our own actions, or are we going to be a pawn to the opinions of others?

In response to the people's request, Aaron told them to give him their jewelry and he would make an idol for them. So, they gave him their jewelry, and he made them an idol shaped like a calf, to which they responded, "'O Israel, these are the gods who brought you out of the land of Egypt,'" (Exodus 32:4). This is a ridiculous statement because the golden calf idol did not do anything to free the people from slavery – a few minutes ago, it had been jewelry. Now they were worshiping their melted jewelry formed by Aaron into the shape of a cow. But Aaron continued to play out this charade, scheduling a feast day to honor their new god.

Later when Moses returned with the original tablets of the Ten Commandments, he was shocked and angered by what he saw. In his reaction to the people's idolatry, "He threw the stone tablets to the ground, smashing them at the foot of the mountain," (Exodus 32:19). Then, "He took the calf they had made and burned it. Then he ground it into a powder, threw it into the water, and forced the people to drink it," (Exodus 32:20). But when Moses confronted Aaron, Aaron offered this excuse: "'They said to me, "Make us gods who will lead us. We don't know what happened to this fellow Moses, who brought us here from the land of Egypt".'" (Exodus 32:23). So far, so good – Aaron is sharing the truth of what happened. But Aaron continued his story: "'So I told them, "Whoever has gold jewelry, take it off." When they brought it to me, I simply threw it into the fire – and out came this calf!'" (Exodus 32:24). Let's examine this claim as if we were confronting Aaron: *OK. Let me get this straight. You threw a bunch of jewelry into a fire and out popped this golden calf? That is your story?!*

This is a case of a leader playing the role of a victim to peer pressure. Instead of owning up to a time of failed leadership, Aaron made up a lame story indicating that he was not at fault – he was a victim to the people's desires and the creative energy of a bonfire. As a result of his actions, "the LORD sent a great plague upon the people because they had worshiped the calf Aaron had made," (Exodus 32:35). People died due to Aaron's weak leadership. Victors are strong leaders; victims are weak leaders if they lead at all.

Leadership is more about influencing others to achieve a common goal than it is being coerced by public opinion to please a mob. Let's take an example from the world of sports. Throughout the years, there have been accusations raised against various baseball teams that they have stolen the other team's pitching signs. Imagine that you were managing a baseball team and someone told you they could decipher the other team's signs. In that case, your batters would know what pitch to expect. Would you justify stealing signs as a part of the competition? It is too late to pretend that you don't know what is happening.

Let's add some more heat to the situation. The owner and the general manager know that you have obtained information that gives you an advantage over the other team, and it is critical for you to win this game so that you can clinch your division title. The owner and the general manager strongly hint that if you do not use this information and the team loses the game, it will cost you your job. Now you are tossed into a situation in which you can be a victor on the baseball field, but it will force you to abandon your moral compass. What are some of the possible actions you could take in this situation? You could be like Aaron, bow down to peer pressure, and do something that you know is not right. You could try to rationalize your cheating by saying that you were just trying to keep your job. Or you could adopt a victor's attitude and seek to win or lose the game based on talent alone.

Leadership involves more than power over people; it also encompasses responsibility and accountability for one's actions. All leaders fail at some point. Strong leaders admit their shortcomings and move forward to overcome their failure. Weak leaders view problems as someone else's fault, and they never admit and overcome their faults and failures. Sometimes weak leaders blame the influence of others for their mistakes. (Sounds similar to Adam's predicament in the Garden of Eden, doesn't it?) In such a case, the person has abandoned their leadership post to play the victim card. Playing the victim card is a losing hand for anyone to play.

CHAPTER 8

Nadab and Abihu:
The Cost of Ignoring God's Instructions

Have you ever had someone close to you mess up their lives in such a drastic way that it resulted in their deaths? It is hard to witness such a tragedy. When it happens, we are confused and seek to find a way for it to make sense. The closer the relationship, the more we feel impelled to deflect any blame from them, even if deep down we know that their deaths were their own fault. We tend to want to soften the tragedy, but we must respond in a compassionate way that also honors the truth.

In Leviticus 8-9, we read the details of the consecration of Aaron and his sons as priests of Israel. The chapters emphasize the holiness of the office of priest, and the prescribed details of worship. The Holy Spirit outlines in painstaking detail the holiness and solemnity of the priesthood. Instead of following God's instructions, Aaron's sons, Nadab and Abihu, decided to make up their own rules for worship. They "put coals of fire in their incense burners and sprinkled incense over them. In this way, they disobeyed the LORD by burning before him the wrong kind of fire, different than he had commanded" (Leviticus 10:1b). Their actions were similar to a person who receives intensive job training but decides to perform their work according to their own rules, even though it puts their life at risk.

God cares about our worship and desires it to honor Him, not ourselves. As a result of the disobedience of the sons of Aaron, "fire blazed forth from the LORD's presence and burned them up, and they died there before the LORD," (Leviticus 10:2). Were the sons of Aaron victims of a tragic event, or were they responsible for their demise? They were clearly not innocent bystanders; they intentionally defied God's guidelines for worship. Moses knew it, and said to Aaron, "'This is what the LORD meant when He said, "I will display My holiness through those who come near Me. I will display My glory before all the people,"'" (Leviticus 10:3a). Aaron knew this truth and remained silent.

Moses gave instructions to Aaron and his remaining sons on how they should respond to the deaths of Nadab and Abihu. He told them not to publicly mourn, even though people outside the family could mourn (Leviticus 10:6). He told them, "'you must not leave the entrance of the Tabernacle or you will die,'" (Leviticus 10:7a). Furthermore, Moses told Aaron not to deaden his pain with alcohol: "'You and your descendants must never drink wine or any other alcoholic drink before going into the Tabernacle. If you do, you will die,'" (Leviticus 10:9). God identified the reason for these restrictions: "'You must distinguish between what is sacred and what is common, between what is ceremonially unclean and what is clean. And you must teach the Israelites all the decrees that the LORD has given them through Moses,'" (Leviticus 10:10-11).

In this passage, there are two major lessons that are passed on to us. First, we need to follow God's instructions for life. For example, a pastor who uses his position of authority to seduce women in his church is well aware of what he is doing if he has a basic level of biblical literacy. So, if he is using his status of pastor to satisfy his sexual desires, he knows that he is ignoring God's instructions regarding sexual morality – he is ignoring God's instructions. He, in good conscience, cannot play the victim card. There is no acceptable "whoops" moment for deliberately confusing things dedicated to God and things dedicated to the world. It is blatant sin to confuse the two. The victim card has no power or influence when a person confuses the holy and the profane.

Second, we need to learn from our mistakes and the mistakes of others. Throughout time, wise younger siblings have avoided much trouble by observing the misdeeds of their older siblings. If an older sibling is caught stealing a ring from a store, and the parents discover the theft, the parents will probably be upset and confront the child about this sinful act. If the child lies to them about the theft even though the parents have solid evidence to prove it, then the parents might become increasingly angry, and the consequences for the child might worsen. The wise and attentive younger siblings learn lessons from their older sibling's mistakes: Admit it when you do something wrong – lying makes it worse. It is foolish to disregard such information and wind up in the same uncomfortable circumstances. When a person ignores previously made mistakes, it is as if they have already read the script and know how the scene will play out, but refuse to say the lines as written and lead the whole scene into chaos.

Our lives are impacted not only by our own struggles, but by the struggles of loved ones. We must not try to change the script and whitewash the sins of those who are close to us, even though that may be our desire. A victor remembers that there are consequences for sin. In addition, gains can be made through negative circumstances if we are willing to learn from them. There is a cost to ignoring God's Word and life lessons.

CHAPTER 9

Achan:
When the Spoils of
Victory Lead to Defeat

Several times I have experienced a wonderful victory in life that was quickly followed by a terrible defeat. There seems to be no consistent reason for this pattern of events. Sometimes, my pride was the reason for my downfall. At other times, I have remained humble and still experienced the sting of defeat. The important thing to remember when you experience the roller-coaster ups and downs of life is that when Jesus is your Lord and Savior, your life is headed toward ultimate victory.

One of the most surprising and unusual military victories in history – the destruction of Jericho – was followed by one of the most shocking defeats in history – the defeat at Ai. Prior to the destruction of Jericho, the people were told that the victory looting had limits: "'Everything made from silver, gold, bronze, or iron is sacred to the LORD and must be brought into his treasury,'" (Joshua 6:19). What most of the Israelite people did not know about were the actions of a man named Achan who ignored the ban on looted items. However, God knew what Achan had done, and "the LORD was very angry with the Israelites," (Joshua 7:1).

Neither Joshua nor any other leader seemed to be aware of Achan's sinful action, so they set their sights on the next town to be conquered in the Promised Land. Joshua sent out spies to the town of Ai to bring back a reconnaissance report. The spies returned and reported, "'There's no need for all of us to go up there; it won't take more than two or three thousand men to attack Ai. Since there are so few of them, don't make all our people struggle to go up there,'" (Joshua 7:3). However, the men of Ai routed them, so that "the Israelites were paralyzed with fear at this turn of events, and their courage melted away," (Joshua 7:5b).

Joshua turned to God in prayer, and God answered by giving him general information regarding the sin that led to their military defeat. The next day, God revealed the specifics of Achan's sins, and Achan received a swift execution. Following these actions, the LORD said to Joshua, "'Do not be afraid or discouraged. Take all your fighting men and attack Ai, for I have given you the king of Ai, his people, his town, and his land,'" (Joshua 8:1). God also gave Joshua a brilliant military strategy that involved his army faking a retreat to open up an ambush from behind the city. Ai was soundly defeated once sin was removed from the Israelite's camp. Joshua and his troops could have become paralyzed by fear after their defeat, but instead they sought after God to restore their blessings.

Notice that the sin that was revealed was an individual's sin, but it affected everyone around him. The consequences of sin often appear to be contagious – they easily infect others. For instance, if a man who is a husband and father becomes dependent on alcohol, then the people around him also suffer the consequences of his addiction.

His wife does not want to enable him, nor does she want to ruin him. If he is a mean drunk, then confrontation could become dangerous. His children do not really get an opportunity to know their dad; they only know a man controlled by alcohol. In this family dynamic, the head of the household is frequently incoherent, which contributes to a chaotic household.

The people he works with have to hear his every-morning complaints of headache and body pain. The workflow in the office is disrupted by his sluggishness and extra-long lunch breaks. His thinking is sometimes unclear, and his memory is faltering. Everyone in the office is impacted in some way by one man's drinking problem.

Let's bring in the focus of this book: Does this man have to continue to live as a victim to his addiction, or can he live as a victor over his addiction? He has a choice to be a victor rather than a victim. The story of the Israelites' victory after defeat reveals exactly what that choice entails. Once they recognized and removed sin, God led the Israelites to victory. Likewise, if the man realizes the reason for his life of defeat – alcohol addiction – and removes it, he can live a victorious life. It may not be easy, but choosing to go down the pathway of healing and restoration leads to victory, as opposed to the path of being a victim to alcohol dependency, which leads to defeat. The Israelites experienced victory over an army that had previously defeated them when they dealt with the sin in the camp. We all face various struggles in life. We might even try to hide them like Achan, and others may suffer as a result. However, if we repent and overcome our struggles, then our victory in these areas positively impacts those around us. None of us has to remain defeated by our mistakes – victory can be on the horizon.

CHAPTER 10

Caleb:
A Life-long Devotion to Victory

At some point, we face circumstances in which we are correct on an issue but overruled by the majority regarding the proper course of action. It is both frustrating and encouraging to know that you are trusting God even though the people around you are not. It is frustrating because you know the right action to take, but your opinion is drowned out by those who lack faith. It is encouraging because you realize that you are in tune with God even though those around you are not. How does this frustration affect our future thoughts and actions? Do we allow our motivations to be controlled by the voices around us, just a victim to the majority? Or do we continue to seek to do right, no matter what the people around us are saying and doing – living and acting like a victor?

It can be hard to continue living as a victor when everyone around you is identifying as a victim – but it is possible, as Caleb shows us.

Not too long after the miraculous parting of the Red Sea, God told Moses to send spies into the Promised Land to bring back a report to the people (Numbers 13). One man was selected from each tribe to be a part of this covert operation. The twelve men went into the land and came back with a report in two parts. First, they stated that the land was even more fantastic than they had anticipated. Second, they reported that the inhabitants were too intimidating for them to invade the land. The vote among the spies was split 10-2 in favor of not invading the land that God had promised them. Ten of the spies were already living with a victim mentality, while two of the spies were confident that they were on the side of God and were therefore would-be victors.

Fast forward about 40 years, and we see that one of the two men who had resisted the majority opinion was now the man who succeeded Moses in leadership: Joshua. The other man, Caleb, was the only remaining spy allowed to enter the Promised Land. When it came time to divide the land into territories for each tribe, Caleb asked for the most dangerous portion of the land grants. He said to Joshua, "'give me the hill country that the LORD promised me. You will remember that as scouts we found the descendants of Anak living there in great, walled towns. But if the LORD is with me, I will drive them out of the land, just as the LORD said,'" (Joshua 14:12). The Anakim were the same people group that the rest of the spies had feared forty years before. The Jewish people believed that the Anakim were descendants of the Nephilim, a fearsome people group who dominated the pre-flood world. Joshua granted Caleb the land that he requested. In case you think the threat had dissipated over the years, the chapter ends with these words: "Previously Hebron had been called Kiriath-arba. It had been named after Arba, a great hero of the descendants of the Anak," (Joshua 14:15a). So Caleb's faith was so great in God's promise of victory that he not only chose to enter a land with dangerous opposition, but specifically chose the most dangerous part of it all! When we focus on trusting God's promises and calling, everything that seems to promise us defeat falls away. When our focus is on God's victory rather than on the obstacles in the way – that's how we can live as victors.

Have you ever known someone who could not be stopped from achieving something that God had promised them? Such a person usually inspires us with their integrity and faith. At Northeastern Baptist College, where I teach, I am surrounded by faculty and staff that exhibit Caleb-like characteristics.

First of all, we are a Christian college in Vermont – one of the least religious states in America. Indeed, Bennington, Vermont is probably one of the last places that a person would expect to find a Christian college. It is not easy, but we keep moving forward.

Second, each faculty member signs an annual contract, but is made aware that their pay is contingent on contributions from donors. One of the surprising things about our college is that students who attend and work twelve hours a week for the college are charged no tuition. We do not want students to go into debt through student loans, so we allow them to pay their tuition through their hard work. This is a great deal for students but makes it challenging to pay the faculty. Personally, it was a difficult decision for me to resign from a position as a full-time pastor receiving regular paychecks to become a full-time professor and occasionally receive paychecks. In this financial challenge, my faith in God has grown. God has been faithful – my family has been able to purchase a home and pay our monthly bills. Just as Caleb trusted God would make a way because He called the Israelites to the land of Caanan, we trust that God will provide for us because He called us to be a part of what He is doing in Bennington, Vermont. The faculty and staff at Northeastern Baptist College desire to have faith like Caleb – always seeking victory and refusing to act like a victim – and you can too. Sometimes it feels like there are giants in the land, but we know that our God is bigger. To God be the glory.

CHAPTER 11

Samson:
Trading Victory for Victimhood

Have you ever met someone who seemed to have everything they needed to be successful in life, yet they made foolish decisions and ended up living a superficial, miserable life? Some people seem to have it all, but they act like all they need is a little more. They seem to have a victorious life, and then they end up playing the part of the victim. As the saying goes, they snatch defeat from the jaws of victory. Samson was such a person, and as a result, he was not able to truly enjoy the blessed life he had been given.

Samson's birth was miraculous and clearly an act of God's blessing to his parents. His mom had been unable to conceive, so his parents thought they would never be parents. But the angel of the LORD appeared to her and said, "'Even though you have been unable to have children, you will soon become pregnant and give birth to a son,'" (Judges 13:3). This child would be a special child. The angel continued his message: "'So be careful; you must not drink wine or any other alcoholic drink nor eat any forbidden food. You will become pregnant and give birth to a son, and his hair must never be cut. For he will be dedicated to God as a Nazarite from birth. He will begin to rescue Israel from the Philistines,'" (Judges 13:4-5). Samson was born to be a holy man of God and defeat Israel's enemies.

As he reached adulthood, Samson's lust for women overpowered his devotion to God. To make matters worse, he had notoriously bad taste in women. For example, he fell in love with a woman named Delilah, whose allegiance to him was clearly questionable. She was pressured by some powerful Philistine men to find a way to overpower Samson's tremendous strength. Her first approach was not subtle: "'Please tell me what makes you so strong and what it would take to tie you up securely,'" (Judges 16:6). Instead of breaking off the relationship, Samson decided to play along and make up a story about how he could be captured: "'If I were tied up with seven new bowstrings that have not yet been dried, I would become as weak as anyone else,'" (Judges 16:7). She tied him up and yelled that the Philistines were coming after him, and he snapped the ropes like dried twigs. In most cases, the man in such a situation would be upset with his girlfriend for trying to get him captured by his enemies. Not so in this weird relationship – she was the one who was offended because he had lied to her. So Samson made up another scenario in which he could be captured, and she tried it out on him with the result of another failure. This pattern kept repeating: she asked him how he could be captured, he made up a story, she tried it, and it did not work. Either Samson never figured out what she was doing, or he did not care that he had a traitorous girlfriend.

Finally, her constant barrage of requests wore him out – "he was sick to death of it," (Judges 16:16b). In a moment of mental weakness, he told her the truth regarding the way he could be physically weakened. She once again followed his instructions, but this time the Philistines captured him, gouged out his eyes, and bound him in prison.

The Bible does not provide any internal conversations Samson may have had while he was in the prison cell or describe how foolish he must have felt. It simply states: "before long, his hair began to grow back," (Judges 16:22). As his strength returned, he developed a plan for his revenge on the Philistine leaders. However, this plan would cost him his own life. Indeed, the plan worked, and Samson killed more people in this act of suicidal revenge than he had killed in the rest of his life.

Samson was born with a holy calling and was clearly blessed by God with great strength. He was selected by God to rescue Israel from their enemies before he was even conceived. He had everything he needed to be a national hero. He had everything he needed to live a life that honored God. He is the kind of guy who could have lived his whole life as a victor. However, he had some serious character defects that led him to suffer as a victim: he was vengeful, lustful, self-centered, and foolish. Every now and then we hear a story on the news about a person who has the same self-destructive traits as Samson. The story usually begins with them becoming a darling of the media and people admiring them. This happens in a variety of ways, but it usually involves them being attractive, successful, or both. We follow them through their books or shows or Instagram. There are usually some warning signs that their life is built on a flimsy foundation, but we often ignore these indicators. Eventually their lives come crashing down, and we are shocked for a while, but then they are easily forgotten.

A similar pattern can be observed in Christian circles when a Christian singer, preacher, or celebrity gains thousands of followers. Everyone admires them and their talents and wants to hear their testimony about Jesus in their life. Later, some of these Christian role models abandon the Christian faith. Just like Samson, they have had a holy calling and have known the blessings of God, but they abandon these good things to chase after the desires of the world.

We must make sure that we don't fall into the same trap. The attractions of this world can be tempting, and they can disorient us from our holy calling of following Jesus and trusting Him. Like Samson, we have been given much that we do not deserve, but that is the meaning of grace – we get what we don't deserve. Let's not abandon God's calling and purpose in our lives: "For we are God's masterpiece. He has created us anew in Christ Jesus, so we can do the good things he planned for us long ago" (Ephesians 2:10).

CHAPTER 12

Naomi:
Hard Times Give Way to Hope

Tragedies can change aspects of an individual's personality. For example, someone who is usually optimistic can become pessimistic after facing a series of crises in life. This change of personality can remain to the extent that the person views life through a pessimistic lens, or the person can return to their previous optimistic one. We see this trajectory of an individual's personality when we look at the life of Naomi as depicted in the book of Ruth.

The biblical story of Naomi's life began with her husband, two sons, and a famine in the land of Judah. Naomi's family traveled from Judah to Moab, where her sons got married, but then her husband and sons died. After this series of losses, Naomi decided to return to Judah because news had traveled that God had

broken the famine there. Both daughters-in-law decided to travel with her, but Naomi convinced one of
them to remain in Moab. The other daughter-in-law,
Ruth, was firmly committed to traveling to Judah and
remaining with Naomi. She said to Naomi, "'Don't
ask me to leave you and turn back. Wherever you go, I
will go; wherever you live, I will live. Your people will
be my people, and your God will be my God. Wherever you die, I will die, and there I will be buried. May
the LORD punish me severely if I allow anything but
death to separate us,'" (Ruth 1:16-17). This is as strong
a statement of personal dedication as we often hear at
wedding ceremonies.

So both women traveled to Judah, but it was
evident that Naomi was not the same person that
she was before she went to Moab. In fact, she wanted to change her name to better fit her new personality: "'Don't call me Naomi... call me Mara, for the
Almighty has made life very bitter for me,'" (Ruth
1:20). "Mara" means "bitter" which is the new way
that Naomi responded to life. Clearly, Naomi's name
change to Mara shows that she identified as a victim.

Back in Judah, Ruth met one of Naomi's relatives on her husband's side of the family: a wealthy
landowner named Boaz. Boaz figured out who Ruth
was and decided to be generous to her by providing
ample food for her and Naomi. When Ruth returned

home and showed Naomi the food given to her by Boaz, a glimmer of hope began to sweeten Naomi's bitterness.

Naomi came up with a plan for the relationship between Ruth and Boaz to become more than platonic. (See chapter 3 in the book of Ruth for the details.) One important detail in this plan was the practice of a family member acting as a "kinsman-redeemer" for a widow in the family. A kinsman-redeemer was a male relative who had the privilege or responsibility to act for a relative who was in a desperate situation. Spoiler alert: Naomi's plan succeeded, at least initially. Boaz was interested in marrying Ruth, but there was a closer relative who had first choice in this situation. Boaz arranged a meeting with this man, and the man decided that he was not interested in serving as the kinsman-redeemer for Ruth. So, Boaz and Ruth got married and had a son. The neighbor women gave him the name of Obed (which means "worshipper") and celebrated: "'Now at last Naomi has a son again,'" (Ruth 4:17). The book ends with a genealogical list from Perez to David, who would be Israel's greatest king. In the end, a sad story of loss ends with a hopeful story of new life and redemption.

It is interesting how aspects of our personalities change according to our circumstances. Sometimes physical circumstances, such as illness, injury, or hunger, can change our personality in negative ways. For example, if I make a snippy remark to my wife, she often assumes that I am hangry (anger fueled by hunger). She is often correct. Even optimists can lose their sunny disposition when they encounter one letdown after another. For example, I have seen Christians who are usually filled with hope become discouraged due to financial difficulties or severe medical issues. Like it or not, our personalities are often impacted by our circumstances. The good news is that we can overcome our circumstances by trusting God in the hard times. Even in our darkest times, God is working. The Bible states: "We know that God causes everything to work together for the good of those who love God and are called according to His purpose for them," (Romans 8:28).

Naomi had become a bitter woman, but her story ends in Ruth with an optimistic outlook for the future, because a son had been born that would be the grandfather of a great man, David. As we explore this genealogy further through the first chapter of the gospel of Matthew, we find that this baby mentioned in Ruth is also linked to the birth of the Messiah, the hope of the world – Jesus Christ!

CHAPTER 13

Hannah:
The Power of a Heart-felt Prayer

It is frustrating and heartbreaking when a woman wants to have a child but is unable to get pregnant. The frustration and heartache increase when the women around her start having babies. Perhaps all her friends are having children, but she is unable to have any. It is easy for her to feel like she is a victim due to her reproductive problems, while her friends are victors, having babies and watching their families grow. Such soul-deep pain is best addressed through prayer to our living God. He can answer prayers by working miracles in which He provides infertile women with children. But if that is not His will, He can comfort the broken hearted as they pour out their hearts to Him in prayer.

In the opening chapter of 1 Samuel, we find Hannah, who is married to a man named Elkanah, who is also married to another woman named Peninnah. In that culture, it was permitted for men to have more than one wife, although it always came with lots of problems. To add to Hannah's feeling of defeat, she was unable to have children, while the other wife, Peninnah, was able to have children. The husband favored Hannah and sought to bless her and take care of her. However, year after year, as they approached the house of the LORD, Hannah would be verbally bullied by Peninnah. These repeated and agonizing confrontations led Hannah into a state in which she felt so defeated that she would not eat; she would just cry.

Hannah could have easily remained in the role of the victim, but her relationship with God would not allow her to give up hope. She reached out to God for help in her despair through prayer. She made a vow to God: "'O LORD of Heaven's Armies, if you will look upon my sorrow and answer my prayer and give me a son, then I will give him back to you. He will be yours for his entire lifetime, and as a sign that he has been dedicated to the LORD, his hair will never be cut,'" (1 Samuel 1:11). Eli, the priest, was watching her, and saw her lips moving but heard no sound because she was praying from her soul (the source of her pain). He thought she was drunk and rebuked her, but she stated her innocence and told him that she had poured out her soul before the LORD. The priest responded, "'Go in peace! May the God of Israel grant the request you have asked of him,'" (1 Samuel 1:17). Hannah felt better after her conversations with the LORD and the priest, probably feeling less like a victim and more like a victor.

Shortly after this event, Hannah became pregnant and gave birth to a son whom she named Samuel. The name "Samuel" means "asked of God" (1 Samuel 1:20b). God had given her a son! Hannah did not return to the house of the LORD until after she had weaned Samuel. She kept her promise to God and brought him to the house of the LORD after he was weaned. This had to be a tough action to carry out, but she had promised God that if He gave her a son, she would give him back to Him. She brought the boy to the priest Eli and told him, "'Sir, do you remember me?... I am the very woman who stood here several years ago praying to the LORD. I asked the LORD to give me this boy, and he has granted my request. Now I am giving him to the LORD, and he will belong to the LORD his whole life,'" (1 Samuel 1:26-28). Praise the Lord for His provision and the way He answers our prayers!

It is emotionally devastating for a couple to desire children but be unable to conceive. Just as Hannah sought an answer from God, so do many couples today. My wife and I experienced this difficulty, and often sought the Lord in prayer. After sixteen years of marriage, we decided to adopt. We would not have waited so long to adopt except for my hesitancy. What changed my mind? I went to a seminar for clergy on the subject of helping infertile couples understand their options. My conclusion after the presentation was that, unless a couple would not be satisfied without biological children, I would recommend that they adopt. I applied this insight to my life and told my wife about it, and she was thrilled. We were turning a corner from feeling like childless victims to planning on adopting children into our family.

A few days later, I was working on a sermon when I experienced a severe case of writer's block. My mind became fixated on one thought: *We should adopt two children.* The idea was crazy to me at the time because it had taken me sixteen years to be comfortable with adopting one child. But nothing I did removed the statement causing the writer's block. So, I prayed something like this: "Lord, I don't know where this idea of adopting two children is coming from, but if it is from You, please forgive my lack of faith. I feel the need to 'lay out a fleece' like Gideon. If adopting two children is from You, then lead Gina to make such a statement to me. I had never heard her specifically say she wanted <u>two</u> children." After I prayed, the writer's block lifted, and I continued to work on my sermon. About twenty minutes later, Gina came home, entered my office, and said to me, "Do you know what I was thinking on the way home? We should adopt two children!" We celebrated the moment like we had just won the Super Bowl! Our attitudes about having a family had shifted from hopelessness to hopefulness. It was clear that God had spoken to us regarding our desire for children. Indeed, despite many obstacles, we adopted a brother and sister from Ukraine, referred to by the Ukrainian judge who approved our adoption as "Jewels of Ukraine."

We all face unmet desires in life. Sometimes the heartache is so severe that we fall into a state of depression in which we don't want to do anything. Often times, one of the things that we do not want to do is pray. But if we can overcome our resistance to prayer, then we can see God work in ways that will astonish us. Hannah had unmet desires to have a family, so she prayed to God for a son, and God gave her one. She didn't hold on to the identity of a "barren woman," but sought God's help and became a mom. Similarly, my wife and I had unmet desires to have a family, so we sought the LORD. He blessed us with not just one, but two children. When we trust God in our struggles, God can bring about victory in our lives, whether it comes about as we had imagined it, or in some other way that might surprise us.

CHAPTER 14

David:
Waiting on God's Promise

It is an honor to be chosen to lead a group of people, but such an honor can come with unexpected troubles. Imagine that you are selected to be not just a leader, but a king, and the first conflict that arises is that the present king is still on the throne, and your personal ethics lead you to honor him as long as he lives. In such a situation, you can fall from the hope of reigning as king to wondering if or when you will get your chance to lead. It can seem like the situation is completely out of your hands and you are stuck with an unfulfilled promise. A choice must be made: Are you going to view this situation as a failed promise (a victim's worldview) or as pending promise (a victor's worldview). King David vacillated between these two positions as he waited for his chance to be king.

In those days, the people of Israel demanded a king so that they could have a government structure like the countries around them. God gave them the kind of king they wanted, although he was not the kind of king that they needed. Saul, the first king of Israel, made many foolish mistakes. As a result, the prophet Samuel declared to Saul, "'Since you have rejected the LORD's command, he has rejected you as king of Israel,'" (1 Samuel 15:26b). The LORD sent Samuel to the family of Jesse in Bethlehem to find the new king. To everyone's surprise, David, the youngest son, was chosen and anointed to be king of Israel. However, there was no impeachment process; King Saul would not be removed from office except by death. David had been anointed as king in a victorious moment but was unable to serve as king for an indefinite length of time. Saul was still the king, and David refused to kill Saul so that he could be king. He had to wait until Saul's life was over. Such a situation is frustrating and can dash the hopes of a victor and make him feel like a victim.

Saul knew that his days were numbered as king, but he did not know the identity of his replacement. Unbeknownst to Saul, he met David, his replacement, but did not know that David had been anointed to be king of Israel. He was impressed by the young man David, especially when he defeated a giant named

Goliath who had been intimidating the entire army of Israel. Afterwards, Saul sent him on military missions, and he was always victorious. Saul's relationship with David began to sour when the king heard a chant or chorus sung by some of the Israelite women: "'Saul has killed his thousands, and David his ten thousands,'" (1 Samuel 18:7). At this point, Saul became angry and jealous toward David, and several times tried to kill him. Once, he threw a spear at David while David was playing the harp for him. Thankfully, his spear missed the mark. Another time, Saul gave David the impossible task of killing one hundred Philistines and bringing back their foreskins as evidence, all for the privilege of marrying his daughter. David accomplished this difficult task, and "when Saul realized that the LORD was with David and how much his daughter Michal loved him, Saul became even more afraid of him, and he remained David's enemy for the rest of his life," (1 Samuel 18:28-29). David had proven himself as a victorious warrior fighting for the kingdom, but his victories stoked the fires of hatred in King Saul. King Saul tried many tactics to victimize David, but none of them worked.

Eventually, King Saul's main mission in life became focused on killing David. In Saul's pursuit of David, there were two clear opportunities for David to reverse the scenario and kill Saul. On the first occasion, David and his men were hiding in a cave, and Saul entered the cave to urinate. David's men encouraged him to kill Saul in this moment, but David refused, saying, "'The LORD forbid that I should do this to my lord the king. I shouldn't attack the LORD's anointed one, for the LORD himself has chosen him,'" (1 Samuel 24:6). David verbally confronted Saul but did not physically attack him, even when he had the advantage. David's attitude showed respect and devotion to God's ways, even when they were inconvenient for him – that is the attitude of a victor.

The second opportunity to kill Saul occurred as the two groups camped in the wilderness. Saul set out to kill David with three thousand of his finest soldiers. One night, as Saul and his army slept, David and one of his men snuck into their camp and got close enough to Saul to kill him. Instead of killing Saul, David spoke to him, "'This very day you can see with your own eyes...the LORD placed you at my mercy back there in the cave. Some of my men told me to kill you, but I spared you. For I said, "I will never harm the king – he is the LORD'S anointed one." Look, my father, at what I have in my hand. It is a piece of the hem of your robe! I cut it off, but I didn't kill you. This proves that I am not trying to harm you and that I have not sinned against you, even though you have been hunting for me to kill me,'" (1 Samuel

24:10-11). David made hard decisions and persevered in his calling from God because he believed that God would make it happen at the right time. His circumstances indicated that his identity would always be as a victim to a vengeful king. However, his faith in God helped him maintain his integrity and his anointing as king. Indeed, King Saul eventually died in battle, and David became king.

How did David display such patience in the face of persecution? He was able to display victory because he knew that ultimately the victory was his. God had told him that he would be king, and he trusted that victory would come. He did not have to panic as someone without hope. David knew that God was sovereign, so there was no reason for David to take control of the situation – he was going to let God fight his battles. When you let God fight your battles, you live as a victor, not a victim. God is undefeated. Even at times when it looks like the forces of evil will be victorious, God claims victory. The best example is the crucifixion and resurrection of Jesus Christ – the ultimate Victor!

CHAPTER 15

David:
Repenting Like a Victor

Even the best of people mess up sometimes. Other than the God-man Jesus, nobody who has walked on this planet has lived a sinless life. King David is described as a man after God's own heart (1 Samuel 13:14, Acts 13:22), but the Bible does not cover up his sins in order to make him look like a great king. At times in David's life, it seemed like he was just a victim to the circumstances around him, sometimes due to his sinful decision making. But David did not let those moments define him. In his weakest moments, he realized his faults, expressed his sorrow to the LORD, and turned away from his sinful actions.

The problems in David's life started when he was not where he was supposed to be, and not doing what he was supposed to be doing. David stayed home at a time when it was customary for kings to go out to battle with their troops. Instead, David was walking around on the roof of the palace when he saw a woman bathing. Instead of diverting his attention from her, he inquired regarding her identity. Someone told him that it was a woman named Bathsheba, who was the wife of one of his soldiers, a man named Uriah. Instead of discarding this information, he had some of his messengers bring her to him. Going even further, he slept with her, and she became pregnant.

When we commit a sin, we can either admit it and repent, or try to cover it up. Victors admit their sins and repent; victims are spiritually paralyzed by their sins. David opted for the cover-up by devising a plan in which her husband would be removed from the battlefield so that he could come home and sleep with his wife. Then the pregnancy could be easily explained as Uriah's. The problem with this plan is that Bathsheba's husband refused to sleep with her when he came back. Since his troops were in the field, he did not feel right being in the comfort of his own home, but slept where the servants slept. The next plan was to get him drunk so he would not hold such high morals and concerns about others. Indeed, he got drunk but still refused to sleep in his house and again slept where the servants slept.

Finally, David decided to arrange for Uriah to be a wartime casualty. He instructed his top general Joab to place Uriah on the front lines of the fiercest battle front, and then retreat – leaving Uriah overwhelmed by the enemy. This time, David's plan worked, and Uriah was killed. After Bathsheba had mourned for her husband a respectable amount of time, David brought her into his house and made her his wife. Nobody would be the wiser to his grand scheme – or so he thought. David thought at that moment that he was a victor but would soon find out that covering up sin victimizes a person.

God would not allow David to stay in the spiritual paralysis of his victimhood. He sent the prophet Nathan to David with a story about two men. One man had one precious lamb that he loved like a daughter. The other man was wealthy and had many flocks and herds. However, when a traveler visited the rich man, he was unwilling to sacrifice one of his own animals, so he took the other man's single, precious lamb and sacrificed it to feed the visitor. After David heard the story, he was infuriated with the rich man's actions: "'As surely as the LORD lives... any man who would do such a thing deserves to die! He must repay four lambs to the poor man for the one he stole and for having no pity,'" (2 Samuel 12:5-6). Nathan said to the king, "'You are that man!'" (2 Samuel 12:7a). That stinging rebuke was aimed at David's heart like an arrow shot from a bow.

How a person responds to being caught in such a sin displays their deeper character. Everyone is a sinner; not everyone is a repenter. After being confronted by Nathan, David admitted, "'I have sinned against the Lord,'" (2 Samuel 12:13a). What kind of actions did David take in repentance? We have some knowledge about David's thoughts and actions because he wrote a song about his need for forgiveness from God: Psalm 51. In the first four verses, David admitted his wrongdoing to God and asked for compassion. He continued to admit his sinfulness and begged for God's grace and mercy. He made a request to God: "'Create in me a clean heart, O God. Renew a loyal spirit within me,'" (Psalm 51:10). He was desperate for his sins to be forgiven and his relationship with God to be restored. He was tired of being a victim to his sins and ready to be a victor over his sins.

Victors and victims react differently when their sins are made public. Victors turn away from their sins and turn towards God. Victims blame someone or something else for their sinful actions. Victors point out their sins and pray to God, "Restore to me the joy of Your salvation," (Psalm 51:12a). Victims point to someone else and say, "It is not my fault; it is their fault."

Lately, as I have watched the news, I have been astonished at the number of American politicians who portray themselves as victims instead of victors. You don't believe me? When was the last time you heard a politician of either party admit that they made a mistake and describe their plan to make amends and get the country moving in the right direction? King David did that, but few leaders do so today. There is something admirable in someone who makes a mistake, owns their responsibility for it, and makes it right. That is what victors do.

CHAPTER 16

Elijah:
Eroding Faith Slips into Victimhood

As we have seen before, life's best moments are often followed by life's worst moments. It is a steep drop when you go from a mountaintop experience to a dark valley in a relatively short time. The emotional and spiritual turbulence arises from the disparity of celebrating the power and presence of God in the good times but doubting the power and presence of God in the bad times. Living as a victor in good and bad circumstances comes from a mindset that God is present and sovereign in all circumstances. We must avoid being "fair weather" followers of God, and instead trust Him in the wonderful and the difficult.

In the situation discussed in this chapter, a prophet named Elijah was to settle a conflict with the king, by way of a spiritual duel. Just prior to the duel,

Elijah had met another follower of God who informed him that he was not the only prophet of God left. The man said to Elijah, "'Has no one told you, my lord, about the time when Jezebel was trying to kill the LORD's prophets? I hid 100 of them in two caves and supplied them with food and water,'" (1 Kings 18:13). The man left and let the king know that Elijah was waiting to meet him.

The conflict between the king and Elijah would be settled by a sort of competition between Elijah and the prophets of the false god Baal. The ground rules were summed up in the following statements: "'Now bring two bulls. The prophets of Baal may choose whichever one they wish and cut it into pieces and lay it on the wood of their altar, but without setting fire to it. I will prepare the other bull and lay it on the wood on the altar, but not set fire to it. Then call on the name of your god, and I will call on the name of the LORD. The god who answers by setting fire to the wood is the true God,'" (1 Kings 18:23-24a).

Elijah let the Baal prophets go first. No matter what they tried to do, no matter how much they cried out, not a single spark was ignited on their altar. When it was Elijah's turn, he was so confident that his God would be victorious that he created a situation in which it would be impossible for any person to light the fire – he made a trench around the altar and flooded the altar with water three times. Then he prayed, "'O LORD, God of Abraham, Isaac, and Jacob, prove today that you are God in Israel and that I am your servant. Prove that I have done all this at Your command. O LORD, answer me! Answer me so these people will know that you, O LORD, are God and that you have brought them back to yourself,'" (1 Kings 18:36-37). Then the LORD sent fire that consumed the offering, the wood, the stones, and the dust, as well as the water in the trench. The LORD was the clear Victor! The Bible describes the response of the witnesses: "When all the people saw it, they fell face down on the ground and cried out, 'The LORD – he is God! Yes, the LORD is God!'" (1 Kings 18:39). After their god's defeat, the prophets of Baal were slain, but Elijah's victory party was cut short by Queen Jezebel declaring his death sentence.

Although Elijah had trusted the LORD in his contest with the Baal prophets, he lacked faith in God protecting him from the queen. Indeed, the plunge from victor to victim can be swift! In his despair, Elijah journeyed into the wilderness and wanted to die. Instead of dying, he slept and woke up to the touch of an angel telling him to get up and eat. This process was repeated, and then Elijah traveled to Mount Horeb. While Elijah was hiding in a cave, God told him: "'Go out and stand before Me on the mountain,'"

(1 Kings 19:11a). Forceful natural wonders occurred on the mountain, including a destructive wind, an earthquake, and a fire, but it was not in those moments that Elijah encountered God. Instead, there came a gentle blowing breeze, and God asked Elijah, "'What are you doing here, Elijah?'" (1 Kings 19:13). Just like with Adam and Eve and Cain, this question was about something deeper than physical location. God was addressing Elijah's spiritual location – where he was in his relationship with God. And just like with the others, God knew the answer, but asked so that Elijah could realize where he was and what he was doing.

In response, Elijah shared his erroneous belief that he was the only prophet honoring the LORD, even though he had been told differently. He also whole-heartedly feared the queen's threat to take his life, which on the surface appeared valid. However, if the context of the victory of Mount Carmel was remembered and applied to the situation, the belief in the queen's death sentence would seem to be an unnecessary stressor. In this moment, God gave Elijah several instructions and corrected his view, sharing that there were actually 7,000 prophets remaining "'who have never bowed down to Baal or kissed him,'" (1 Kings 19:18a).

Why do we jump to false conclusions in difficult circumstances that decrease our faith in God and cause us nothing but stress? One reason is that we become controlled by the fear of possible outcomes, instead of trusting in our sovereign God. For example, an empty-nester Mom might feel called to go to college and start a new career, but her fears of failure may keep her from attending. But if she considers this opportunity from the perspective of a victor and recognizes God's leading in this endeavor, she knows she can overcome her fears.

Related to fear is a lack of faith that God is really leading in a new and unexpected way, or that He is even capable of leading in an unexpected way. The mom may sense that God is leading her to start a new career but lacks faith that God can equip her to accomplish such a feat. She says to herself, "I am too old to learn new things. What if I am misunderstanding what God wants me to do?" Questioning God's call can paralyze someone from responding in obedience and result in a victim mentality. On the other hand, viewing herself as a victor would lead her to know that if God has called her, He will equip her. As is often noted, God equips the called; He doesn't call the equipped.

Sometimes our faith is weak because we are simply worn out. For example, if the mom had homeschooled each of her three children, and the youngest one just graduated high school, then she may be too tired to believe that God could start anything new in her life. Before Elijah could get to a place where he could hear and accept what God was trying to tell him, he was first made to rest and eat. Sometimes just taking some time to rest can help us escape a victim mentality. Our enemy does not like to see us victorious in Jesus' name. He will try to discourage us in any way that he can. We must be more convinced by God's work than we are of the devil's lies. We must remember the victories that God has brought before, rest so we can hear from him again, and see our situation more accurately. These are choices that will keep us living as victors.

CHAPTER 17

Elisha:
Trusting in the Unseen

Having an understanding of God's presence and activity around us helps us live as victors instead of victims. Sometimes our minds are so distracted by what we see that we forget that God is working in the unseen realm. Our perspective on circumstances is revealed by our focus on either the seen (material things) or the unseen (spiritual things).

The prophet Elisha was a faithful messenger of God. When he received a message from God, he shared it with confidence. For example, while war raged between the nations of Aram and Israel, Elisha provided tactical intelligence to the king of Israel as he received it from God. The king of Aram was not immediately aware of Elisha's role but thought there must be a betrayer among his servants. One of his servants told him that the information leak was the prophet Elisha of Israel. So one night, to capture him, the king: "sent a great army with many chariots and horses to surround the city," (2 Kings 6:14).

In the morning, one of Elisha's assistants woke up, ventured outside, and saw the army encircling the city. The servant found Elisha, told him what he saw, and asked what action should be taken in light of their vulnerable situation. Elisha's answer shocked his servant because it did not seem to match the circumstances: "'Don't be afraid!... For there are more on our side than on theirs!'" (2 Kings 6:16). From a physical standpoint this statement made no sense. As the servant looked around him, he saw a vast enemy army surrounding them, but no army on their side. From all appearances, they were in a hopeless situation, but Elisha was focused on what God was doing in the unseen spiritual world, so he was able to take the perspective of a victor. Then Elisha prayed for his servant to see the things that existed in the spiritual realm, and "he saw that the hillside around Elisha was filled with horses and chariots of fire," (2 Kings 6:17b). Upon Elisha's request, the LORD struck the Aramean army with blindness. Then Elisha led the blinded army to Samaria, and there released them. Because of this, "the Aramean raiders stayed away from the land of Israel," (2 Kings 6:23b). The unseen forces of God routed the enemy soldiers trying to kill Elisha. He was a victor in a situation that looked like he would be a victim.

Most of us know the verse: "We walk by faith, not by sight," (2 Corinthians 5:7 ESV). This is one of those verses that is much easier to memorize than it is to actualize. We have to train and focus our minds on the truth of this verse and trust God, as did Elisha and his servant. Let's apply this truth to the following scenario. A man named Larry is blessed with a good family and a successful career as a local businessman. God is blessing Larry and his family in every way imaginable. Life is happening as if it were following a Hollywood script. Then something happens that knocks Larry off-kilter: his pastor abruptly resigns from his church. As the congregation is seeking God's leading for a new pastor, early in the process several of the members sense that God is calling Larry to step up in that way. There is some hesitation among some of the pastor search committee because Larry has no Bible college or seminary training – he has been trained to be a businessman. But after weeks of prayer and discussion, the group agrees that, despite his lack of theological education, God is calling Larry to be their new pastor. Larry has not applied for the position or expressed interest, but the committee unanimously agrees that he is the one God is calling.

You can imagine the shock Larry experiences when a couple of the members of the search committee show up at his house one Tuesday night and tell him all of this. Larry is completely stunned. He didn't see it coming. He didn't seek the position. He feels unqualified and overwhelmed by even the thought of being a pastor. He tries to convince the men that they are mistaken, but they are insistent that he is the man for the job.

Later, as Larry discusses the church's offer with his wife, she seems less surprised than he expected. She has been watching her husband grow spiritually and has noticed that God has blessed him with the spiritual gifts, temperament, and compassion necessary to be a pastor. With her eyes on the unseen, she encourages him to seriously consider the offer. After weeks of prayer, Larry can't explain it logically, but he senses that God is calling him to shepherd the church as pastor. He feels totally overwhelmed but trusts God and steps out in faith.

There are often times in each of our lives in which we are following God's will the best that we can but feel overwhelmed by the physical circumstances around us. We must not let those feelings burden and bury us, or else we will give up and feel defeated. Instead, we must remember that there are spiritual forces at work which we cannot see. When we realize the spiritual firepower around us, we step out in faith and are able to live as victors. God has saved us, called us, equipped us, and now He is fighting our battles. Trust and thank God for the victories in your life.

CHAPTER 18

Nehemiah:
Focusing on Godly Success

For many reasons, Nehemiah is one of my favorite characters of the Bible. A brief analysis of his life is fitting in a book about choosing to live as a victor or a victim. We can relate to Nehemiah's story when we have a desire to fix a major problem, but the solution seems out of our reach. If we do begin to make progress, there are always those who want to impede our achievements. Often our opponents are crafty and persistent, and the process can be draining. Despite the feelings of being overwhelmed and ridiculed, a victor continues to move forward step-by-step. A victim gives up, abandoning the project and resuming their previous life patterns, and usually ending up in a rut of defeats and frustrations.

Nehemiah's story begins with him receiving bad news about his ancestral home, Jerusalem: "'Things are not going well for those who returned to the province of Judah. They are in great trouble and disgrace. The wall of Jerusalem has been torn down, and the gates have been destroyed by fire,'" (Nehemiah 1:3). This bad news disturbed Nehemiah to the core of his being. His first response should be the first response of everybody who trusts in God – he prayed.

While Nehemiah was in this season of praying for Jerusalem, his deep concern was evident by his facial expressions. His employer, the King of Persia, noticed his sadness and asked him to tell him about his troubles. Nehemiah explained that the news regarding Jerusalem was devastating to him. After some discussion, the king agreed to let Nehemiah return to Jerusalem and even gave him official documents to provide safety and building materials.

When Nehemiah arrived in Jerusalem, he covertly surveyed the condition of Jerusalem and found that it was just as bad as he had heard. He had a decision to make: abandon a hopeless project or trust in God for success. Nehemiah opted to trust God and gave a short speech to the people. He told them about the favor that God had already bestowed on the rebuilding of Jerusalem. When the people heard Nehemiah's words, they were motivated to join him in rebuilding the wall. However, not everyone was pleased – there were some outside the people of Judah who opposed the effort and characterized it as a rebellious act against the king. Such opposition did not much faze Nehemiah and his victor mentality.

Nehemiah developed a genius plan to assign portions of the wall to be rebuilt by specific groups (see Nehemiah chapter 3 for the details). Their enemies lodged a negative campaign against it characterized by such statements as, "'That stone wall would collapse if even a fox walked along the top of it!'" (Nehemiah 4:3). How should we respond to such criticism? Sometimes we get upset and quit, and at other times such words encourage us to work harder. Which option sounds like the victor and which sounds like the victim? Clearly, victors who are following the will of God choose to work more diligently in the face of opposition.

The next strategy of Nehemiah's enemies involved physical threats: "'Before they know what's happening, we will swoop down on them and kill them and end their work,'" (Nehemiah 4:11). So, Nehemiah instructed his workers to be vigilant and productive: "The laborers carried on their work with one hand supporting their load and one hand holding a weapon," (Nehemiah 4:17). Again, the enemy's tactics failed to distract the people of Jerusalem from building the wall around their city because victors do not give up in the face of adversity; they plow through it.

The next trick up the sleeve of the enemy was to seek a "reconciliatory" meeting. Nehemiah's response to this meeting is one of the best responses ever made: "'I am engaged in a great work, so I can't come. Why should I stop working to come and meet with you?'" (Nehemiah 6:3). The enemy kept trying to distract Nehemiah from his God-given assignment, but remarkably, the wall around Jerusalem was completed in just fifty-two days. Notice how it affected their enemies: "When our enemies and the surrounding nations heard about it, they were frightened and humiliated. They realized this work had been done with the help of our God," (Nehemiah 6:16). The achievements of a victor who is serving God are unsettling to their opposition because they realize that they are not battling against a person, but ultimately against God.

Some Christians assume that any opposition that they face is a message from God informing them that they are not in His will. Most of the time, opposition indicates a much different reality: The enemy is trying to stop you from doing God's will. Let's say that a man and his wife feel God is leading them to leave their hometown in Georgia and plant a church in a town in Vermont that has no Bible-believing church.

Vermont is often identified as the least religious state in our country, so this is a challenging assignment for a church planter. Is the church-planting couple likely to face many different types of opposition? Yes. Does the opposition mean that they are outside of God's will? No, especially if God called them to plant a church in that town. Like Nehemiah, the task might seem impossible, but God often makes apparently impossible things possible. Like Nehemiah, there might be all kinds of threats and distractions, but a victor remains focused on their God-given task and perseveres until the impossible is not just possible but accomplished. Like Nehemiah, a victor needs to remain focused on God working and bringing the victory.

CHAPTER 19

Job:
Victory Despite Losses

What do you do when you are on top of the world one moment and in the next moment you feel crushed by your circumstances? Do you play the role of a victim and look for someone to blame? Or do you play the role of a victor and try to figure out what you did wrong, going to God with your frustrations? These are questions that might seem easy to answer for the armchair quarterbacks of life, but they are more challenging for people who face them in real life. Job was a man who struggled with some of these questions, but ultimately was the victor.

The book that bears Job's name describes him as "blameless - a man of complete integrity. He feared God and stayed away from evil," (Job 1:1). Not only that, but he was also blessed relationally with a big family and blessed financially with many possessions. But one day, the enemy of God-fearing people, Satan, made a bold claim to God that Job only honored God due to His blessings in his life. The devil thought if the blessings were removed from his life, Job would curse God. This theory has proven true in some people throughout history, but it was not true for Job. His response to his losses was: "'I came naked from my mother's womb, and I will be naked when I leave. The LORD gave me what I had, and the LORD has taken it away. Praise the name of the LORD,'" (Job 1:21). In a moment of terrible tragedy, Job refused to play the victim and instead trusted in God. Everyone else around him in the seen and unseen world, excluding God of course, expected him to be crushed by his losses and curse God. Job's faith in God enabled him to remain a victor in a time of apparent defeat.

Later, Satan again approached God and theorized that if Job's health was compromised, then he would certainly curse God. God knew Job's faith and permitted Satan to attack his health, but not take his life. As a result, the devil "struck Job with terrible boils from head to foot," (Job 2:7). In his agony, his wife said to him, "'Are you still trying to maintain your integrity? Curse God and die!'" (Job 2:9). When your closest relationships fail to encourage you, it can be tempting to grab hold of the victim card. Yet Job refused to curse God. He refused to wallow through the remainder of his life as a victim.

Some of Job's friends came to comfort him, and they did a good job of it until they opened their mouths. Then they began to berate Job to confess his sins that must have led to his troubles. But remember that God's Word states that Job was blameless, upright, fearing God, and turning away from evil. Also remember that we know a part of the story that was unknown to Job and everyone around him – Job's problems were due to satanic attacks.

Throughout much of the book of Job, his "friends" try to convince him to repent of his sins despite the fact that his problems were not due to sin. At any time in this process, Job could have given up and lived a hopeless and helpless life. Instead, he pleaded for God to answer his prayers. God did answer Job's prayers...but not like Job expected. God's answer made clear His omnipotence, omniscience, and omnipresence, and pointed out the finiteness of Job's understanding. Job got the message, as indicated by his concluding remarks: "'I had only heard about you before, but now I have seen you with my own eyes. I take back everything I said, and I sit in dust and ashes to show my repentance,'" (Job 42:5-6). God restored Job's blessings, and Job humbled himself before God and continued to live out his identity as a victor due to his relationship with Him.

Sometimes church members might look at the circumstances of your life and exhort you to confess your sins and repent – assuming that your difficulties are due to your sinful thoughts or actions. Sometimes they will be correct because you have made poor choices that have led to the challenging consequences you now face. Other times, like Job, you have done nothing wrong but are suffering from the actions of someone else. We must have the discernment to know if we are playing the role of sinner or sufferer.[2]

Let me share an example from my life. One of my vocational dreams was to be a college professor, but I assumed that such an opportunity would never come because there are countless more qualified people than me to teach at a college. Imagine my surprise when I was at a leadership conference and was asked by an acquaintance if I would consider teaching at a new Christian college in Vermont: Northeastern Baptist College. I told him I was very interested and appreciated the offer. Nothing was finalized, but it was decided we would follow up with this opportunity after the conference.

The next Sunday, I was letting our geriatric dog, Kasey, outside early in the morning. We had a ramp that led from our front door stoop to the yard be-

2   Emlet, Michael R. *Saints, Sufferers, and Sinners: Loving Others as God Loves Us.* Greensboro, NC: New Growth Press, 2021..

cause Kasey was starting to have mobility issues. It had snowed just enough to cover the ground the previous night. As I stepped onto the ramp, I slipped and fell flat on my back, breaking my neck. I could have viewed this unexpected injury as an omen not to seek the college teaching position, but I didn't see it that way. All I saw was the abundant and awesome mercy of God. You see, there is a part of the story that I have not told you. After falling, I laid on the ramp for a few minutes with the thought that I had been seriously injured even though I felt no pain at the time. I had learned earlier in life that a person with a spinal injury should not be moved or it could result in further injury. I don't know why, but I disregarded this information and crawled into the house on my hands and knees, greatly alarming my wife. Most of the medical personnel who heard this story responded with a statement like, "I don't know why you are not dead or paralyzed." My answer: God's mercy. Mercy is evident when we don't receive what we deserve to receive. I knew better than to move, much less to crawl into the house, but I did it anyway. This terrible injury was not God's retribution for my decision to teach at the college; instead it displayed God's mercy for a foolish man. Now I am living the dream and teaching Christian counseling classes at Northeastern Baptist College! God is good!

None of us are immune to struggles in life. What makes the struggles of life more intense are those times when we did not do anything to bring the consequences upon ourselves but are experiencing suffering due to the sins of others or the effects of spiritual warfare. It is easy to adopt a victim mentality when we are suffering from someone else's actions, but such thinking stunts our spiritual growth. As long as we think of ourselves as victims, we are stuck in our circumstances. Adding to the struggle, people can sometimes "pile on" with hurtful comments about our need to repent when we have done nothing wrong. It would be easy to collapse into a heap and give up, but that is not a victor mentality. To think and act like a victor, we need to dig down deep in our souls and know that God is all-knowing, all-present, and all-powerful. He does not discipline those who are suffering; He comforts those who are struggling. Instead of pushing us down, He lifts us up out of the pain we experience and gives us confidence to live as victors because we belong to Him.

CHAPTER 20

Shadrach, Meshach, and Abednego:
Living with a Win-Win Attitude

Picture a scene in which a governmental leader does not want the people in his country to focus on God, but on him. So, he persecutes church leaders and followers of Jesus in his attempts to shut down the competition. How does a follower of God respond when a government leader oversteps the bounds of their authority? It would be easy to play the role of the victim and conform to the leader's dictates – in private complaining about the situation, and in public going along with the crowd. The problem is that the leader wins, but the individual loses. How can a person avoid living as a victim in a hostile political culture? More importantly, how can a person live as a victor by standing up for their beliefs despite the consequences? It can be a win-win situation when a person does the right thing and ends up with a positive result. These are not only increasingly relevant issues, but they are situations found in the pages of Scripture.

The Bible records a historical event in which King Nebuchadnezzar of Babylon made an image of gold that had to be worshiped when music was played. Due to widespread fear of King Nebuchadnezzar, most everyone complied with the king's new law. However, three captured Jewish men refused to bow down to the golden image, and news of their rebellion reached the king. The three men were not willing to give up their beliefs to go along with the crowd because the end result would be them losing their freedom to worship God. Nebuchadnezzar confronted the men, whose Babylonian names were Shadrach, Meshach, and Abednego. He offered them a second chance to bow down before the idol or be burned to death in a furnace. The king then asked a question that he probably thought was rhetorical: "'what god will be able to rescue you from my power?'" (Daniel 3:15b). At this moment, the men could have dropped their objections to the king's demand for them to worship an idol, or they could continue to defy the king's order and in so doing trust God in the situation. Buckling under political pressure would make them lose their distinctiveness as followers of the one, true God.

The Hebrew men did not need much time to ponder the king's orders. They answered: "'If we are thrown into the blazing furnace, the God whom we serve is able to save us. He will rescue us from your power, Your Majesty. But even if he doesn't, we want to make it clear to you, Your Majesty, that we will never serve your gods or worship the gold statue you have set up,'" (Daniel 3:17-18). The king was furious and demanded that the furnace be heated seven times more than it was usually heated. He had the Jewish men bound so they could be cast into the furnace. But the furnace was so hot that the men carrying the Jewish men were themselves killed by the heat. Eventually, Shadrach, Meshach, and Abednego were thrown into the deadly furnace. The king remained as a spectator and was shocked to see a fourth person walking in the furnace with them, and that none of the men in the furnace were suffering any harm. The fourth person looked "like a god," (Daniel 3:25b). In response to what the king was seeing, he ordered the three men out of the furnace. The government officials at the site inspected the men and found that "the fire had not touched them. Not a hair on their heads was singed, and their clothing was not scorched. They didn't even smell of smoke," (Daniel 3:27). It is miraculous that the blazing fire had no impact on them or even their clothes. If you have ever sat around a campfire, you know how likely it is that your hair and clothes will smell like smoke when you leave. The three men had trusted God to give them the victory in this perilous situation, and God kept them from being affected at all by the fiery furnace. It was clearly a win-win situation for them. Instead of being victims to the whims of the king of Babylon, they were victors through the King of Kings.

This miraculous event so shook the king that he proclaimed a blessing on the three Jewish men even though they had defied his authority. Then the king went a step further and made it illegal by penalty of death to say anything offensive about the God of Shadrach, Meshach, and Abednego. This historical account ends with these words: "Then the king promoted Shadrach, Meshach, and Abednego to even higher positions in the province of Babylon," (Daniel 3:30). The king had a definite change of mind after he saw the one, true, living God's protection and provision for the young men who trusted Him.

During the recent Covid pandemic, governmental leaders and agencies forced the closings of schools, businesses, and churches. Severe restraints were placed on public gatherings of worship. For example, the state of California limited places of worship to 25-50 percent capacity, depending on the location. When churches were allowed to meet together, singing was banned, or at least strongly discouraged. Most churches complied with the decrees and guidelines. However, Grace Community Church in Los Angeles refused to bow down to the mandates of the state. County officials sued the church to require it to comply with the Covid guidelines, however the church continued to resist the restrictions on worship gatherings. Influenced by a recent Supreme Court decision, the county officials later changed their minds and agreed to pay Grace Community Church a total of $800,000.[3] The pastor, John MacArthur, the staff, and the members held tightly to their right to congregational worship and experienced victory in a time when victimhood was the expected outcome. Grace Community Church followed the example of the Hebrew youth who were willing to suffer the consequences for their disobedience to the king. In both cases, the worshipers of God trusted that God was with them and even if they could not see Him there with them, they would trust Him and not bow down to a government that was trying to control worship. The Hebrew youth and Grace Community Church had the mindset of a victor, even when it caused hostility between them and the government. They knew that if they honored God, He would take care of them, a win-win situation.

---

3   https://www.christianitytoday.com/news/2021/september/john-macarthur-covid-settlement-california-church-grace-com.html.

CHAPTER 21

Daniel:
Victorious in the Face of Workplace Conflict

Throughout history, there have been two types of people who seek to advance in the workplace. One type of worker focuses on doing the job to the very best of their ability. They usually do not compare the quality of their work with the quality of their co-workers' work – they leave the evaluations to their supervisors. They have a victor mentality – they believe their best efforts lead to success. The other type of worker tries to make themselves look good by making their coworkers look bad. They do their job, but they also spend time strategizing ways to bring down those who seem to be favored by the supervisors. They have a victim mentality – they believe that their lack of success is someone else's fault. In this chapter, we will see a situation in which victims try to destroy victors.

Daniel was a man who had been uprooted from his home country and taken into forced exile in the foreign nation of Babylon. He did not choose to go to Babylon, and he was there with no chance of leaving. Many of the cultural practices of Babylon were offensive to his values. For example, the diet that was offered to him and his Jewish friends did not comply with the Jewish dietary laws, so it was unclean. Demonstrating a victor's mentality, "Daniel was determined not to defile himself by eating the food and wine given to them by the king. He asked the chief of staff for permission not to eat these unacceptable foods," (Daniel 1:8). This was a bold request from someone who was a prisoner to the king. In negotiations between Daniel and the chief of staff, Daniel and his Hebrew friends offered to be part of a dietary experiment: "'Please test us for ten days on a diet of vegetables and water... At the end of the ten days, see how we look compared to the other young men who are eating the king's food. Then make your decision in light of what you see,'" (Daniel 1:12-13). The chief of staff agreed to the experiment, and at the end of the testing period, all the young men were brought before the king. "The king talked with them, and no one impressed him as much as Daniel, Hananiah, Mishael, and Azariah," (Daniel 1:19a). From this glimpse into Daniel's character, it is obvious that Daniel was a victor who excelled in everything that he did.

Due to his character and intelligence, Daniel found career success in the country of his exile. Even more impressive is the fact that Daniel found favor from the king who conquered the Babylonians, King Darius the Mede. Just as before, "Daniel soon proved himself more capable than all the other administrators and high officers. Because of Daniel's great ability, the king made plans to place him over the entire empire," (Daniel 6:3). Within the government, workplace rivalry clearly existed. In this case, Daniel's peers and competitors knew that the only way to discredit Daniel would be to find some accusation against him. Try as they might, they could not dig up a single thing he had done wrong. So, they decided to entrap him by passing a law that they knew he, in good conscience, could not keep. They passed a law that if anyone was caught praying to anyone or anything other than the king, they would be thrown into the lions' den as a death sentence. They saw themselves as victims of Daniel's success, so instead of working harder, they tried to remove Daniel from his place of authority.

Sure enough, even though Daniel knew about the law, he also knew he could not obey it. As was his custom, he prayed to God and was caught in the act by the conspirators. When Daniel was arrested and charged, the king had no option but to enforce the law, although it grieved him to do it. This added another "victim" character, the king who had signed a law that he could not remove. In that culture, a law, once signed, could not be revoked, even by the king.

Daniel was cast into the lions' den, and the king said to him, "'May your God, whom you serve so faithfully, rescue you,'" (Daniel 6:16b). The lions' den was sealed for the night with Daniel inside it. How would you feel if you were Daniel and were being thrown into the lions' den even though you had done nothing morally wrong? What emotions and thoughts would be racing through your mind? Daniel had the mindset of a victor, and he maintained his character and trusted God in his circumstances.

The next morning, the king hurried to the lions' den and yelled for Daniel. He was surprised and pleased when Daniel responded, saying, "'My God sent His angel to shut the lions' mouths so that they would not hurt me, for I have been found innocent in his sight. And I have not wronged you, Your Majesty,'" (Daniel 6:22). Daniel was lifted up out of the den, and the king ordered the conspirators against Daniel to be thrown into it instead. Before the bodies of the conspirators hit the floor of the den, the lions killed them.

Have you ever had a job in which it seemed like your co-workers were trying to make you look bad so they could look good -- instead of trying to outwork you? This is a troubling work environment, but for someone with a victor mindset, it can be just a minor annoyance. Picture this scene: You just moved to a new town and were hired by a department store. The employees at the store are not too friendly toward outsiders because they feel threatened by their presence. You are a hard worker, and your work ethic is noticeably different than the other workers'. The other employees begin to respond to you in a hostile way, but you treat them with kindness and respect. They keep reporting you to the manager for the slightest discrepancies – nobody is perfect. The manager sees beyond their petty actions and appoints you as assistant manager, which sends the other employees to a victimized frenzy. Just like the story of Daniel, victors achieve while victims attempt to deceive.

CHAPTER 22

Jonah:
Finding Misery in God's Blessings

Sometimes people feel victimized by God. How does a person get into this mindset? Often, it begins with a strong personal opinion about something that differs from God's perspective on the issue. Our personal desires can sometimes be so strong that we try to rebuke God for failing to give us what we want. However, we are fighting a battle that we cannot win. The more we persist in trying to do things our own way, the more we will face defeat, because we cannot defeat God. It is better to humble ourselves, repent, and join God for the victory than it is to let your pride turn you into a victim.

The prophet Jonah had a strong prejudice against the people of Nineveh: that they were not worthy of an evangelistic campaign. So, when it turned out that

God wanted Jonah to go to Nineveh with a message of repentance and salvation for the city, Jonah rebelled against Him by getting on a ship heading the opposite direction. But God persisted to get Jonah where He wanted him. He sent a storm that was so powerful that the crew panicked and threw all the cargo into the sea. When it continued, they cast lots to determine who was to blame for it, and the culprit was Jonah. Therefore, Jonah was thrown into the sea as a peace offering to the storm. While he was sinking in the water, a great fish swallowed him, and he remained inside the fish for three days. You might argue that if you were in the belly of a fish for three days, you would feel like a victim too. But this important question must be answered: Why was Jonah in the belly of the fish? He was there because he had chosen to rebel against God and to head the opposite way from where God intended him to go. Unfortunately, his choice led him to the gastrointestinal structure of a big fish.

While he was there, Jonah began to return to the LORD and prayed from the belly of the fish. As a result, God commanded the fish to vomit Jonah onto dry land. Then God gave Jonah another command to go to Nineveh. This time Jonah did not run the other way, but neither did he put his heart into the mission. His message was simple: "'Forty days from now Nineveh will be destroyed,'" (Jonah 3:4b). Surprisingly, the entire city responded to this message by repenting of their sins, fasting, and praying to God. God granted their prayer requests and poured out His grace on Nineveh. The whole town responded to the Word of God and were victorious!

This should lead to a happy ending, right? It should, unless you had a heart of stone like Jonah. Ignoring the spiritual awakening in Nineveh, Jonah was angry with God for being gracious and compassionate to the people of Nineveh. Jonah was disappointed that Nineveh was not destroyed. In fact, he was so disappointed that he asked God to strike him dead. In a time of great celebration, Jonah was so self-centered that he played the role of the victim.

The story gets even a little more bizarre. God provided a plant to grow and provide shade for Jonah as he sulked. Jonah loved the plant – in fact, his relationship with the plant was the only positive relationship he had in the book that bears his name. But God sent a worm that killed the plant, and Jonah responded with this depressed sentiment: "'Death is certainly better than living like this,'" (Jonah 4:8b). Sometimes people with a victim mindset get melodramatic. The book of Jonah ends with God making a connection between His compassion for the people of Nineveh and Jonah's compassion toward the weed. We are not told of Jonah's response to this application.

When a person defies God, their relationships with people also suffer. Consider this situation: God gives a man all the spiritual gifts necessary to teach a suburban Bible study. God wants him to teach it in the suburbs, but the man wants to teach it in the city. He might make plans and efforts to teach a Bible study in the city, but God's blessing will not go with him. God may take some extraordinary measures to get the man to lead a small-group Bible study where He wants the group to meet – in the suburbs.

Following the Jonah model, what would you expect after the Bible study leader relented and decided to go where God wanted him to go? He would have a terrible attitude – almost hoping that the suburb Bible-study group fails and disbands so that he can do what he wants to do.

Still following the Jonah model, the Bible study in the suburbs is a huge success, now having to meet in multiple homes. Now the man is mad at God because he did not want these people in the suburbs to have a Bible study. Even in the midst of God's blessings, he would be miserable—such is the victim mindset.

The example of Jonah and the reluctant Bible study leader show us that we can sometimes prefer failure to success when God's way means we don't get our own way. In a weird way, sometimes it may seem like we are competing against God when we hold too tightly to our personal desires. This can only lead to seeing ourselves as victims. God will always be the victor, but we don't have to play the role of the victim. Instead, we can choose to do things God's way and experience victory.

CHAPTER 23

Jesus:
The Ultimate Victor

Sometimes we feel inclined to grant someone a lifetime "victim" card due to the circumstances of their life. If we do this, we are not doing such a person a favor, because we are not letting them rise above victim status. Nobody has to stay in an identity box labeled "victim." When it comes to overcoming life traumas, there is no better example and no greater source of hope than Jesus. The prophet Isaiah record-ed the suffering of the Messiah more than seven hun-dred years before it happened. As we highlight three of the verses of Isaiah 53, think of the ways that Jesus proved victorious over His struggles and sufferings.

Isaiah 53 verse 3 says, "He was despised and re-jected – a man of sorrows, acquainted with deepest grief. We turned our backs on Him and looked the other way. He was despised, and we did not care." The Merriam-Webster Dictionary defines bullying as "abuse and mistreatment of someone vulnerable by someone strong and more powerful." Based on this definition, bullying does not apply to the Suffering Servant. Jesus was much stronger and more powerful than His persecutors, yet He allowed them to inflict harm on Him. In other words, He was willingly reviled, rejected, and insulted.

Moving on to verse 5, Isaiah continues, "He was pierced for our rebellion, crushed for our sins. He was beaten so we could be whole. He was whipped so we could be healed." This verse makes clear the reason for Jesus' suffering – He suffered for us. We can have new life and forgiveness of our sins because He died in our place, taking upon Himself the eternal penalty of our sins. Jesus took the punishment for our sins so that we could spend eternity in heaven with Him.

Finally, in verse 7 we see: "He was oppressed and treated harshly, yet he never said a word. He was led like a lamb to the slaughter. And as a sheep is silent before the shearers, he did not open his mouth." As He was suffering for us, Jesus was not complaining or cursing those who were hurting Him. In other words, He did not act like or identify as a victim, even in the face of death. He suffered mainly in silence for us. Seven brief statements were made during the events connected to the crucifixion. There was no long monologue to explain what He was doing. His actions speak loudly, then and now.

These three verses illustrate a personal hardship for Jesus that outweighs all the struggles in our lives. He was innocent of all the charges against Him but chose to die on that wooden cross anyway. Jesus did not succumb to a sinister plot developed by His enemies. The Bible repeatedly shows how Jesus was the mastermind of His own crucifixion. To spot some indicators of His sovereignty during His suffering, locate the Scriptures in the gospels that speak of Him fulfilling prophecy.

What is even more amazing is the fact that He knew this would happen to Him while He was in heaven, before He came to earth. Remember that these prophetic words were written more than seven centuries before His entrance into Bethlehem. Think about how we would probably respond in His situation. We would either refuse to leave heaven or do everything we could to stop the crucifixion from happening. These types of thoughts were the tools used by the devil when he tempted Jesus in the wilderness. But just as Jesus overcame the devil, so He also resisted all those who tried to change His mind about Him sacrificing His life. Even His own disciples tried to discourage Him from dying on a cross.

He had no Plan B, because there was no other way to rescue us.

The life of Jesus makes it clear that nobody has to hold onto a victim status. We might be victimized at some point in our lives, but it does not have to define us. Those of us who are following Jesus can learn from His love and obedience to the Father how to overcome our most difficult situations in life. Those of you who are not yet following Jesus—He offers you a gift that is so precious. He says to you: "Come to me, all of you who are weary and carry heavy burdens, and I will give you rest. Take my yoke upon you. Let me teach you, because I am humble and gentle at heart, and you will find rest for your souls. For my yoke is easy to bear, and the burden I give you is light," (Matthew 11:28-30). True words from the Ultimate Victor!

ABOUT THE AUTHOR

Dr. George Sweet is a Christian counseling professor at Northeastern Baptist College and the Executive Director of Hope Christian Counseling in Bennington, Vermont. Prior to teaching full-time at the college, he pastored churches in Vermont and Virginia. His wife, Gina, is a science teacher at a Christian school. In addition, he has two grown children, and two grandchildren.

www.ingramcontent.com/pod-product-compliance
Lightning Source LLC
Chambersburg PA
CBHW071155120626
46546CB00006B/2271